PROPHECY
OR
HERESY

**Will Biblical Christians Be Removed
From The Earth To Heaven?**

God's Word vs Man's Doctrine

H. SPEED WILSON
Col. USMC (Retired)

DARING PUBLISHING GROUP, INC.
LIFE ENRICHMENT PUBLISHERS • DARING BOOKS
CANTON • OHIO

Published by Life Enrichment Publishers
P.O. Box 20050, Canton, Ohio 44701

Printed in the United States of America.

All Scripture quotations are from the King James Version of the Bible, unless otherwise indicated as follows: American Standard Version (ASV), Amplified Bible (Amp), Good News (GN), Jerusalem Bible (Jer.), New American Standard (NAS), New English Bible (NEB), New International Version (NIV), New King James Bible (NKJ), Phillips Modern English (PME), Revised Standard Version (RSV) and Rotherham's Emphasized Bible (REB).

Some scriptures have only the key words noted in the text, in the interest of saving space while making a point, however, these are not taken out of context, and the readers are encouraged to look up each of these scriptures themselves to *"see if these things be true!"*

Dedicated to:

SCRIPTURAL TRUTH

and

SOUND DOCTRINE

Table of Contents

Editor's Note

Over the years, there has been much speculation about the rapture doctrine. With the intent of clarifying the issue, many books and magazine articles have been written discussing the who, what, when, why and how *'the rapture'* is to be. To our knowledge, there has been little written challenging the rapture doctrine!

In his book, RAPTURE! PROPHESY OR HERESY, Speed Wilson now pointedly asks the question, *'Is there to be a rapture?'* He proceeds to answer this question using scripture after scripture from the Old and New Testaments. He reveals to the reader that the 'whole counsel' of God's words shows us to be 'overcomers' in the tribulation, not 'copper-outers!'

Speed is so sure that the scriptures disclose there will *not* be a 'rapture', as popularly believed, he offers a $10,000 reward to anyone who can scripturally prove there *will* be a 'rapture', and also answer the scripture references he has cited proving anything other than the 'righteous shall remain' always on Earth.

If you believe in or have been taught by your church, denomination, or pastor there is to be a rapture, we would like you to consider these items:

• This book has not been published to offend you. After receiving Speed's manuscript in 1987 and making note of the fact that he said the much proclaimed rapture date of May 14, 1988 (Israel's 40th anniversary as a nation, seemed like a good date for a rapture!) and the September 12, 1988 date (proclaimed by a popular book in 1988) and others would *not* take place . . . we waited. Sure enough, they did not happen. Then, after a month of studying every scripture and word of Speed's book in five versions of the Bible (King James, New International, Revised Standard, Living Bible and Modern Language) we came to the conclusion that indeed, there was strong scriptural evidence showing the 'rapture' doctrine was false.

- If the rapture is a false doctrine, what *is* the truth for events during the end times? We believe the diligent reader of this book, who is sincerely searching for the truth, will be comforted and awed at the majesty and wisdom the Bible offers through the 'whole counsel of God's word,' not simply a verse or two.

- Though your church or pastor may be sincere and absolutely correct in most of the doctrines presented to you—no man or denomination is ever 100% correct. The only perfect man to ever walk the Earth is Jesus. So, unless you have the point of view as the Apostle Paul who said, "I conferred not with flesh and blood," the only way you can determine if the rapture is indeed prophesied in the Bible, is to read both sides of the issue in the scriptures. Then pray and seek God for your answer.

- The most important point to learn through this book might be to receive the attitude of a famous evangelist's wife, who wrote to a close friend of Speed's and in essence shared this thought, "I no longer personally believe in a rapture, and I would rather be prepared to go *through* the tribulation as an *overcomer*; and, be pleasantly surprised *if* a rapture occurs, than not be prepared for suffering at all."

Think about this. Are we not willing to face trials and tribulations and be overcomers, because the scriptures state many will be 'alive and remain' when Jesus comes again? Are we any less willing to experience persecution, prison—or death—as many thousands of our brothers and sisters have throughout history . . . yea, as even Christ and His disciples suffered?

The facts are, no matter what circumstances we find ourselves facing, we should just *trust* that *Jesus is more than able to keep us* in the midst of evil, and *not test any of us beyond our personal ability to endure?*

We as believers must be willing to say, "Yea, Lord, Thy Will be done, Amen."

-The Editors

1

Rapture?
A Very Important Question

The rapture question is far too important...even critical and urgent, to be ignored by responsible *"apostles, prophets, evangelists, pastors* and *teachers"* (Eph. 4:11). God holds them responsible for the doctrines they proclaim. Jesus said, *"Anyone who shall offend* (deceive or cause to stumble) *one of these who believe in Me, it were better for him to have a millstone* (1,000 pounds plus) *hung about his neck and cast into the sea to drown,"* (Mat. 18:6 and Luke 17:1, 2). However, God also holds each believer responsible to question teachings and doctrines by exorting them *"to search the Scriptures daily to see if these things be true"* (Acts 17: 11). As the apostle Paul truely said, *"...I confer not with flesh and blood..."*

If believers have been taught and believe they will be physically removed from the earth to heaven before the great tribulation in a rapture, then find themselves *in* the great tribulation; they may become prime candidates to be in the *"great falling away,"* (2 Thes. 1, 2, 3 and Dan. 11:35). The Living Bible says it this way: *"And now, what about the coming of our Lord Jesus Christ, and our being gathered together to meet him? Please don't be upset and excited, dear brothers, by the rumor that this day of the Lord has already begun. If you hear of people having visions and special messages from God about this, or letters that are supposed to come from me, don't believe them. Don't be carried away and deceived regardless of what they say."* There have been false prophets throughout history who proclaimed their knowledge of the end of time. However, had the believers been taught and accepted that they should be prepared for *whatever* may come as overcomers, Jesus promised, *"To him that overcometh will I grant to sit with Me in My throne, even as I also overcame,"* (Rev. 3:21), and if a rapture does occur, all is gain, *"He that overcometh shall inherit all things, and I will be his God and he shall be My son"* (Rev. 21:7), with no "falling away."

To blindly accept the doctrine of a rapture, with no consideration of the possibility of God having other plans for his children, may be tempting God. Our Lord Jesus Christ, the Son of God, refused to tempt God when He said, *"It is written,"* (Deut. 6:16), *"Thou shall not tempt the Lord thy God"* (Luke 4:12).

When we recognize the potentially devastating consequences to those who accept the rapture doctrine, we can see how *very* important it is to resolve and answer the question:

Is there to be a rapture?

This question can be resolved *only* from the Word of God, the Holy Bible, the Scriptures.

The rapture doctrine is not taught nor accepted by all who call themselves Christians. Therefore, a brief explanation is in order to gain understanding of the question and to define

8

the term, rapture.

The most widely accepted rapture doctrine has all Biblical believers physically removed from the earth to heaven *before* the Biblically prophesied time of great tribulation, (Mat. 24:21). This is called the pre-trib rapture.

Others read Scriptures they believe make it clear that Biblical believers are *in* the great tribulation. They developed the doctrine that the rapture will occur half-way through the great tribulation, or in the middle of it. This is called the mid-trib rapture.

An increasing number of believers read Scriptures which lead them to conclude that the Biblical believers do not depart this world until *after* the great tribulation. This is called the post-trib rapture.

As the expression goes, ''There are some who believe in the 'pre-trib,' others the 'mid-trib' and others a 'post-trib rapture,' but we can all accept *'pan-trib'*...that is, it will *pan-out* just as God has it planned!'' The purpose of this book is to try to discover God's plan. God's plan is revealed In His Word...the Bible.

Most of the popular books, pamphlets and sermons on the subject of rapture are devoted to *when* the rapture will occur...pre-trib, mid-trib or post-trib...but they do *not* ask the most important, basic question of whether or not there *is* to be a rapture.

Some among those who embrace the pre-trib rapture doctrine have recognized that we are living in prophetic times and calculated the exact date of the rapture. The most popular date was May 14, 1981. This date was derived from the belief that the establishment of the nation of Israel on May 14, 1948 marked the beginning of a Biblical generation of forty years that would see the appearing of Jesus Christ. They believe the duration of the great tribulation is seven years. As pre-tribers, they were to depart in a rapture before the great tribulation. So, they calculated: May 14, 1948 + 40 years (a generation) = May 14, 1988—7 years (of great tribulation) = May 14, 1981.

Another date for the rapture receiving media attention, came from a book devoted to the subject was, April 1, 1980. Considerable media attention was given to a group who sold all their worldly possessions to be ready for the rapture which their leader had calculated would occur June 20, 1981. After that date, they adjusted the date by adding forty days to depart this world on August 8, 1981. In the book, *88 Reasons Why The Rapture Is In 1988,* the rapture was scheduled for September 12, 1988.

Obviously, these prophesied departures from this world enroute to heaven did not come to pass. Jesus told us to expect this just prior to the end of this age when He said, *"And many false prophets shall arise, and shall deceive many,"* (Mat. 24:11).

They could have spared themselves and other believers much embarrassment if they had spent more time determining, from the Holy Scriptures, whether or not there *was* to be a rapture *before* they started scheduling their departure dates.

How big or powerful is your God? If He is powerful enough to physically remove you from the earth and transport you to heaven in a rapture, then He most assuredly is capable of protecting you here on earth to see you through the great tribulation as an *overcomer*. Jesus reassures us that *"...with God all things are possible,"* (Mat. 19:26). Or stated another way, "With God nothing is impossible." If you can really believe that, then you can be at peace and search the Scriptures to learn which God will do...take you out, or see you through!

There are many doctrines which prevent Christians from fellowshipping *"centrally"* (Webster's—equally accessible from various points) in the Lord Jesus Christ. This is reprehensible and confuses the unbelievers. However, the diversities of doctrines most devastating effect is detering Christians from being "made *one* in" the Lord Jesus Christ, to fulfill the prayer of our Lord in John 17:21, *"That they all may be one, as thou, Father, art in me, and I in thee, that they also may be one in us: that the world may believe that Thou hast sent me."* How can the world believe when they see Christians prophesing things that are proven wrong? What would make them see anything different in Christians than in the rest of the world?

The rapture doctrine is one of the most divisive of modern-day doctrines. If this book can help resolve this doctrinal issue, it will be more than justified and will become a blessing. I pray it may be one step toward reducing the confusion and bringing all Biblical believers to knowing the oneness of our Lord Jesus Christ in our "fellowshipping one with another," Amen. *"But if we walk in the light, as He (Jesus) is in the light, we have fellowship one with another, and the blood of Jesus Christ cleanseth us from all sin,"* (1 John 1:7).

2

The Prophetic Words of Jesus

As we become Bereans and *"search the Scriptures daily to see if these things* (in this case, rapture doctrines) *be true,"* (Acts 17:11); we have to accept the fact that the word, rapture, does *not* appear in the text of *any* Bible in *any* language. It appears *only* in footnotes of some, commentaries, etc. In the first two verses of Hebrews we read, *"God, who at various times and in different ways spoke in times past to our fathers by the prophets, has in these last days spoken to us by His Son..."* And in Matthew 17:5 God the Father said of Jesus, *"This is my beloved Son in whom I am well pleased, hear ye Him."* If we believe we are in the "last days," the words of Jesus demand our attention.

In Matthew 24:3, Jesus is asked three questions: When shall the temple be destroyed? What events will occur before

Your coming? What events will mark the end of this age? Jesus answers these three questions in Matthew 24, Mark 13 and Luke 21.

A sudden removal of all true Biblical believers in a rapture would certainly be a most spectacular event (sign) to both those departing and those who remain on the earth. Therefore, we would expect Jesus to include such an event (sign) in His prophetic answers to the questions about the "end of this age" and "His coming." There would certainly be no point in His disguising or hiding such an important thing, after all, why would Christians have to know much about the end of time and the "great tribulation" if we aren't going to be here?

In Matthew 24:37-41, Jesus starts answering the "coming" question: *"But as the days of Noah were, so shall also the **coming** of the Son of Man be. For as in the days that were **before** the flood, **they** (the wicked) were eating and drinking, marrying and giving in marriage, until the day that Noah entered into the ark* (Noah and family entered the ark seven days *before* the flood, Genesis 7:7 & 10). *And (they*—the wicked) *knew not* (Noah *knew*— he built and entered the ark) *until the flood came and took **them** (the wicked) **all away; so shall also the coming of the Son of Man be."***

Before going any further, we must establish beyond any doubt that *"they"* and *"them"* clearly refers to the wicked (ungodly unbelievers) of *"the days of Noah **before** the flood."* If you doubt this, re-read the above passage of Scripture until you clearly see that *"they"* and *"them"* can *only* be referring to the wicked and *not* Noah.

Now that we know *"the flood came and took **them** (the wicked unbelievers) **all away,"*** we continue reading at verse 40, *"Then* (at the coming of the Son of Man) *shall two be in the field, the* (wicked) *one shall be taken, and the other left. Two shall be grinding at the mill; the* (wicked) *one* *shall be taken and the other left."*

In Luke 17:26, 27 and 34-36, we find this record of what Jesus said, *"As it was in the days of Noah, so shall it be also in the day of the Son of Man.* **They** (the wicked) *did eat,* **they** (the wicked) *did drink,* **they** (the wicked) *married wives,* **they** (the wicked) *were given in marriage, until the day that Noah entered into the ark, and the flood came and destroyed them* (the wicked) *all"..."I tell you, in that night there shall be two men in one bed,; the* (wicked) *one shall be taken* (destroyed) *and the other left. Two women shall be grinding together; the* (wicked) *one shall be taken* (destroyed) *and the other left. Two men shall be in the field; the* (wicked) *one shall be taken* (destroyed) *and the other left."*

These prophetic words of our Lord Jesus Christ are taken *out* of context by many who accept, propagate and perpetuate the rapture doctrine to make these verses say it is the Biblical believers who are "taken" and the wicked "left" to endure the "great tribulation." But, when read *in* context, you clearly see the *exact opposite* is the Scriptural truth. Also Peter stated it clearly in 2 Peter 2:5, *"(God) saved* (kept safe) *Noah...bringing in the flood upon the world of the ungodly* (wicked).*"* By taking our Lord's words *out* of context they do violence to God's word!

You may want to know what happens to the "taken ones." So did the disciples of Jesus, and they asked Him in Luke 17:37. He answered, *"Where there is a dead body, there the vultures will gather,"* (New International Version). The King James Version and Revised Standard Version incorrectly translate, "vultures," as "eagles," however, the Revised Standard Version and the American Standard Bible both have a margin note, "or vultures." The following Bibles say "vultures": Amplified Bible, Phillips Modern English, Jerusalem Bible, Living Bible, New American Standard, New English Bible, New International Version, Good News Bible

14

and Rotherham's Emphasized Bible.

As Webster's defines Vulture: a large bird that lives chiefly on carrion (decaying flesh of a dead body). And to further confirm that this is the fate of those who disobey God, we read in Revelations 19:17,18, *"And I saw an angel standing in the sun; and he cried with a loud voice saying to **all the fowls** that fly in the midst of heaven, 'Come and gather yourselves together unto the supper of the great God; that ye may **eat the flesh** of Kings, and the flesh of captains, and the flesh of mighty men, and the flesh of horses, and of those who sit on them, and the flesh of all men, both free and bond, both small and great.'"*

So, these "taken ones" are to "be devoured." Therefore, the "taken ones" *cannot* be the Biblical Christians, because they are to be *"alive and remain,"* (1 Thes. 4:15 and 17 which will be studied in detail later in this book).

Do these "one is taken (destroyed) and the other left" scriptures agree with the prophetic parables of our Lord Jesus Christ?

In Matthew 13:24-30, we read Jesus' prophetic "end of the age" parable of the "wheat and tares" where our Lord says, *"...The Kingdom of Heaven is likened unto a man which sowed good seed in his field: But while men slept, his enemy came and sowed tares among the wheat, and went his way. But when the blade was sprung up and brought forth fruit, then appeared the tares also. So the servants of the household came and said unto him, 'Sir, didst not thou sow good seed in thy field? From whence then hath it tares?' He said unto them, 'An enemy hath done this.' The servants said unto him, 'Will you have us go and gather them up?' But he said, 'Nay, lest while ye gather up the tares, ye root up also the wheat with them. Let both grow together until the harvest: and in the time of harvest I will say to the reapers, 'Gather* together **first the tares**, *and bind them in bundles to burn them: but gather the wheat into my barn."'*

At the request of His disciples Jesus explains this parable in Matthew 13:37-43 saying, *"...He that sowed the good seed is the Son of Man; the field is the world; the good seed are the children of the Kingdom; but the tares are the children of the wicked one; the enemy that sowed them is the devil; the harvest is the end of the world* (age)*; and the reapers are the angels. As therefore the tares are gathered and burned in the fire; so shall it be at the end of this world* (age)*. The Son of man shall send forth his angels, and they will gather **out** of His Kingdom all things that offend, and them which do iniquity, and will cast them into the furnace of fire: there shall be wailing and gnashing of teeth. Then shall the righteous shine forth as the sun in the Kingdom of their Father. He who hath ears to hear, let him hear!"*

It is still so very clear from the parable of the wheat and tares that it is the tares (ungodly) who are destroyed (taken) and the wheat (righteous) left *in* the world. This is exactly as "in the days of Noah." And is in total agreement with the words of Jesus in Luke 17:29, 30 where He says, *"...(in) Sodom it rained fire and brimstone from heaven and destroyed them all. Even thus shall it be in the day when the Son of Man is revealed."*

Jesus continues by giving yet another prophetic parable in Matthew 13:47-50 saying, *"Again, the Kingdom of heaven is like unto a net that was cast into the sea* ("multitudes of people" Rev. 17:15) *and gathered of every kind, which, when it was full, they drew to shore; and they sat down and gathered the good into vessels, but threw the bad away. So shall it be at the end of the world: the angels shall come forth, and sever the wicked from among the just, and cast them into the furnace of fire: there shall be wailing and gnashing of teeth."*

16

Still so very clear that the "good" remain and the "bad" are thrown away..."the wicked" taken/destroyed "from among the just," who remain on the earth.

Paul also tells us in 1 Thessalonians 5:3, *"For when they* (the wicked) *shall say, 'Peace and safety;' then sudden destruction shall come upon them...and they shall not escape."*

After giving these four, very clear examples of who is to be destroyed *out* of the earth and who is to *remain* on the earth, He asks, as He might very well today ask those who embrace the rapture doctrine, *"...Have ye understood all these things?"* I hope you can answer as they did, *"Yea, Lord,"* (Mat. 13:51). *None* of these Scriptures require any interpretation and must not be ignored!

Our Lord Jesus Christ also gives us some prophetic words for the Biblical believers and the great tribulation in His response to the end of the age question, starting at Matthew 24:21, 22 and Mark 13:19, 20 where He says, *"For in those days shall be affliction, such as was not from the beginning of the creation which God created unto this time, neither shall be. And except that the Lord had shortened* (decreased in number) *those days, no flesh should be saved* (survive)*: but for the elect's sake whom He hath chosen, He hath shortened the days."* To understand this we must establish who is referred to as *"the elect."* The following Scriptures make very clear that "the elect" can be no other than the true Biblical believers in the Lord Jesus Christ: Luke 18:7 *"...His* (God's) *own elect...",* Romans 8:33 *"...God's elect.",* Colossians 3:12 *"...the elect of God...",* and Titus 1:1 *"...God's elect..."* If all Biblical believers had been removed from the earth in a rapture *before* the great tribulation, why would God shorten the duration of the "great tribulation for the sake of the elect," (Biblical believers)? The answer is obvious because the elect are *in* the great tribulation! There is no distinction made anywhere

17

here, as some have suggested, that "the elect" are Jewish evangelists, rather, these passages are believed by all to include all believers. So, the pre-trib rapture will *not* survive when exposed to the light of Scripture, without a lot of explaining and interpreting and juggling of terms!

How about a mid-trib rapture? Consider the following prophetic words of Jesus: *"...He that shall **endure** unto the end shall be saved,* (not the "Jew" who endures to the end!) (saved—protected—see Strong's Concordance, word #4982)" Matthew 10:22, 24:13 and Mark 13:13. These three Scriptures leave no doubt that the Biblical believers will be kept safe/protected to go through the great tribulation *as overcomers*, to see the events (signs) that will occur *"Immediately **after** the* (great) *tribulation of those days. Shall the sun be darkened, and the moon shall not give her light, and the stars shall fall from heaven, and the powers of the heavens shall be shaken: And then shall all the tribes of the earth mourn, and they shall see the Son of man coming in the clouds of heaven with great power and great glory. And He shall send His angels with a great sound of a trumpet, and they shall gather together **His elect** from the four winds, from one end of heaven to the other. Now learn a parable of the fig tree; when his branch is yet tender, and putteth forth leaves, ye know summer is nigh: So likewise ye, when **ye shall see all these things,*** (here again, not when the "Jew" shall see all these things) *know that it is near, **even** at the doors."* (Mat. 24:29). No mid-trib rapture! How else could we *"see all these things,"*? Why would Jesus bother to warn us how to tell the end is near, if we weren't going to be here to see all of it? And He said, "after!"

We know from Americans who have been prisoners of war, in the hands of Godless, atheistic Communists, that those who believe in the Lord Jesus Christ for their salvation have survived where unbelievers perished. We have the following

18

wonderful promise from God's Word in 1 Cor. 10:13 (Amplified Bible), *"...God is faithful* (to His Word and to His compassionate nature), *and He* (can be trusted) *not to let you be tempted and tried and assayed beyond your ability and strength of resistance and power to endure..."* This is our blessed assurance that we can go through the great tribulation as *overcomers*.

The Lord Jesus Christ also confirms His above prophesies in a prophetic prayer. Jesus said in John 8:28, 38, *"...I do nothing of myself; but as my Father hath taught me, I speak these things."* So, we can be *very sure* that what Jesus prays will be answered and will come to pass, thus His prayers become prophecy.

In John 17:1, Jesus is praying to the Father God before His crucifixion. In this prophetic prayer we read in verse 15 Jesus said, *"I pray **not** that thou shouldest take them **out** of the world, but that thou should **keep them** from evil."* In verse 20 we find that Jesus is *not* praying just for His disciples when He says, *"Neither pray I for these alone* (His disciples, verse 20), *but **for** them **also** which **shall** believe on Me through their* (the disciples) *word."* Certainly Jesus wouldn't have made one of his last prayers on earth to *keep* believers holy and *not* take them out of the world, if He really meant the opposite. Jesus never *hid* anything from us. Cults, on the other hand, are known for their hidden doctrines!

Are you a believer according to the words (writings) of the disciples of Jesus in the New Testament? If so, then our Lord Jesus Christ is praying the Father God *not* to take us out of the world but to keep us safe *in* the world. Do you doubt that this prayer of Jesus will be answered, be fulfilled and come to pass? Can you really doubt that the prophesies of our Lord will be fulfilled and come to pass? The Lord Jesus Christ is *not* a false prophet!

3

The Law, the Prophets
and the Psalms

In John 10:35, Jesus assures us that *"...the Scriptures cannot be broken,"* (will not disagree nor be in contradiction) and will come to pass (be fulfilled). We are told in 2 Timothy 3:16, *"All Scripture is given by the inspiration of God and is profitable for doctrine, for reproof, for correction and for instruction in righteousness..."* Jesus rebuked the Sadducees, saying, *"Ye do err* (in need of 'correcting') *because you do not know the Scriptures,* (Old Testament) *nor the power of God"* (Mat. 22:29 and Mark 12:24).

It is difficult to understand, but there are some who insist that the Old Testament is not for Christians. By the Word of God in the New Testament, that is *not* true. Romans 15:4, NIV, *"For everything that was written in the past* (Old Testament) *was written to teach US."* 1 Corinthians 10:11, NIV, *"These things happened to them* (people of the Old Testament) *as examples* (and types) *and were written as warnings for us..."* Acts 3:24, NIV, *"Indeed, all the prophets, from Samuel on, as many as have spoken,* (in the Old Testament) *have foretold these days."* Acts 26:22, *"...Saying none other things than those which the prophets and Moses* (in the Old Testament) *did say should come..."* And Jesus tells *us* in Luke 24:44, *"...These are the words which I spake unto you, while I was yet with you, that all things must be fulfilled, which were written in the law of Moses and in the Prophets and in the Psalms* (Old Testament) *concerning Me."*

We are admonished in Acts 20:27, RSV, to take *"the whole counsel of God," not* just the New Testament and *not* just a few verses taken out of context as some who believe the rapture doctrine have done with one is taken/destroyed, the other left Scriptures.

Let us see what we can learn from the whole of God's Word about a rapture from the law, the prophets and the psalms in the Old Testament:

Psalm 125:1, *"They that trust in the Lord shall be as Mount Zion which **cannot be removed,** but abideth forever."*

This agrees with 2 Corinthians 9:9, *"...His (God's) righteousness remains forever."* 2 Corinthians 5:21, *"For He* (God) *hath made Him* (Jesus Christ) *to be sin for us, who knew no sin; that **we** might be made the **righteousness** of God in Him* (Jesus Christ).*"* So we who are to become the righteousness of God in answer to the Lord Jesus Christ's prayer in John 17:21, (I pray) *"That they* (all believers, v. 20) *all may be one; as thou, Father, art in Me, and I in Thee, that they may be one in us."* And of course you remember, *"Christ in you, the hope of glory* (righteousness).*"*

Proverbs 2:21, 22, *"For the upright shall dwell in the land, and the perfect shall **remain** in it, but the wicked shall be cut off **(taken/destroyed)** from the earth and*

21

the transgressors shall be rooted out of it." (This word, remain, appears twice in 2 Thes. 4:15, 17 which will be considered later.)

Psalm 145:20, *"The Lord preserveth all that love him: but all the wicked he will destroy."*

This agrees with 2 Peter 3:7, *"But the heavens and the earth, which are now, by the same word are kept in store, reserved unto fire against the day of judgment and perdition* (destruction) *of ungodly men."*

Proverbs 10:30, *"The righteous shall never be removed; and the wicked shall not inhabit the earth."*

These Scriptures require no explanation nor interpretation!

These Scriptures all agree with the prophetic words of the Lord Jesus Christ. And the Scriptures continue to agree in the following:

Proverbs 11:31, *"The righteous shall be recompensed* (rewarded) *in the* (world) *earth..."*

Psalm 101:8, *"I* (God) *will early* (first) *destroy the wicked of the land..."* (Remember the tares are destroyed first [Matt. 13:30] from among the wheat.)

Psalm 119:119, NIV, *"All the wicked of the earth you discard* (throw away) *like dross."*

Proverbs 25:4,5, *"Take away the dross from the silver...Take away the wicked from before the King..."*

Isaiah 5:24 and 29:5, *"The flame consumeth the chaff* (wicked).*"* This agrees with Mat. 3:12 and Luke 3:17, LB, *"He will separate chaff from grain, and burn up the chaff with eternal fire..."*

Job 21:18, *"They* (the wicked) *are as stubble before the wind, and as chaff that the storm carrieth away."*

Job 38:13 (Speaking to God), *"...take hold of the ends of the earth that the wicked might be shaken out of it."* This agrees with Hebrews 12:27, *"...removing those things that are shaken...that those things that cannot be shaken may remain."*

Malachi 4:1, *"For behold the day cometh...and all that do **wickedly**, shall be stubble: and the day that cometh shall burn them up..."*

Psalm 23:4, 5, *"Yea, though I walk **through*** (no rapture) *the valley of the shadow of death, I will fear no evil; for Thou art with me..."* (Remember Jesus prayed, "Father, do not take them out of the world but keep them from evil" John 17:15.)

Psalm 37:29, *"The righteous shall inherit the land* (earth) *and dwell **therein** forever."*

Psalm 37:9-11, *"For **evildoers*** (wicked) *shall be cut off* (destroyed)*; but those that wait upon the Lord shall inherit the earth. For yet a little while and the wicked shall not be; yea, thou shall diligently consider his place, and it shall not be. But the **meek*** (humble and teachable) *shall inherit the earth* (world)*; and shall delight themselves in the abundance of peace."* No rapture for the meek!

Psalm 37:34-40, *"Wait on the Lord, and keep His way, and He shall exalt you to inherit the land* (world): *when the **wicked*** (tares) *are* (destroyed) *cut off, thou shalt see it. I have seen the wicked in great power* (Rev. 13—The "anti-Christ" system) *and spread himself like a green bay tree. Yet he* (the wicked) *passed **away**, and, lo, he was not; yea, I sought* (looked for) *him, but he* (the wicked) *could **not be found*** (in the world). *Mark the perfect man and behold the upright; for the end of that man is peace. But the transgressors shall be **destroyed together*** (tares gathered together and burned, Matthew 13:40): *the end of the **wicked** shall be cut off* (destroyed). *But the salvation of the righteous is of the Lord: He is their strength **in the time of*** (tribulation) ***trouble.** And the Lord shall help them, and deliver them, He shall deliver them from the **wicked*** (evil one), *and save* (protect) *them, because they trust in Him."* The "righteous, perfect, upright and those who trust in the Lord" are *not* raptured out of the world, but are kept safe and sound *on* the earth!

Psalm 91:7-16, *"A thousand shall fall at thy side, and ten thousand at thy right hand; but it shall not come nigh thee* (near you). (Remember Ez. 9:4, 6 and Rev. 9:4) *Only with thine eyes shall **you see the reward of the wicked.** Because thou hast made the Lord, which is my refuge, even the Most High, thy habitation; there shall no evil befall* (come upon) *thee* (just as Jesus prayed!—John 17:15) *neither shall any plague come nigh thy dwelling. For He shall give His angels charge over you, to keep thee in all thy ways. They* (the angels) *shall bear thee up in their hands, lest thou dash thy foot against a stone. Thou shalt tread upon the lion and adder* (snake)*: the young lion and the dragon* (satan) *shalt thou trample under feet. Because He has set His love upon me* (God) *therefore, will I* (God) *deliver him. I* (God) *will set him on high, because he hath known My name, He shall call upon Me, and I will answer him; I will be with him in* (tribulation) *trouble; I will deliver him and honour him. With long life will I satisfy him and shew* (show) *him My salvation."* (Again, God does not rapture His people out of their tribulation on earth, but sees them through it, and we are here to *see* the punishment of the wicked.)

Isaiah 1:28, *"And the destruction of the transgressors and of the sinners shall be together, and they that forsake the Lord shall be consumed."* And Isaiah 13:9, *"Behold, the day of the Lord cometh, cruel both with wrath and fierce anger...and He shall destroy the sinners thereof **out** of it* (the earth)*."* Also, *"The wrath of God is coming on the sons of disobedience,"* Colossians 3:6.

Isaiah 43:2, *"When thou passest **through** the waters I will be with thee; and **through** the rivers, they shall **not** overflow thee; when thou walkest through the fire, thou shalt **not** be burned; neither shall the flame kindle* *upon thee.''* (And again, we shall be kept safe *in* the world!)

Psalm 104:35, *"Let the sinners be consumed **out** of the earth* (world)*, and let the wicked be no more."* (Jesus said it would be "as in the days of Noah" when the flood took all the wicked away.)

Psalm 52:5, *"God shall likewise destroy thee* (the wicked) *forever; He shall take thee **away**, and pluck thee **out** of thy dwelling place."* (Sounds like Jesus talking about the wicked being taken and the righteous left in the world!)

More than two dozen Scriptures quoted in this chapter make it as clear as it can be stated that the righteous will *remain* in the world and the wicked will be destroyed out of the world. Can you find two dozen Scriptures that state as *clearly* that the righteous will be removed from the world in a rapture? Can you find one? Remember, "clearly" is the key word!

Some of those who have accepted the rapture doctrine might reason and say, "Yes, but these Scriptures on the destruction of the wicked of the earth happen during the wrath of God on the earth *after* the righteous have been 'raptured' up to heaven." We have seen that Jesus said that is *not* so, but let us consider the following Scriptures:

Ezekiel 9:4-6, *"And the Lord said unto him, 'Go through the midst of the city, through the midst of Jerusalem, and set a mark upon the foreheads of the men that sigh and that cry over all the abominations* (sins and wickedness) *that are done in the midst thereof...' 'Go ye after him through the city, and smite* (kill) (destroy)*; let not your eye spare, nor have ye pity. Slay utterly old and young, both maid, and little children, and women; but come **not** near any man upon whom is the* (My) *mark; and begin at My sanctuary.'"*

Does the New Testament agree with this?

Rev. 9:3, 4, *"...and unto them* (locusts) *was given power, as the scorpions of the earth have power. And* *it was commanded then that they should not hurt the grass of the earth, neither any green thing, neither any tree; but **only** those who do **not** have the* (mark) *seal of God on their foreheads."*

Please notice those who do *not* have the "mark of God on their foreheads" are destroyed while they are *still among* those who *do* have God's mark. The righteous remain after the wicked are taken/destroyed from the midst of the righteous, who *remain on* the earth. Just as the wheat and tares and "as in the days of Noah."

God's Word speaks ever so clearly!

Men's doctrines bring confusion!

4

Bible Examples

Remembering that in 1 Corinthians 10:11 God tells us that, *"Now all these things* (testings) *happened unto them* (people of the Old Testament) *as ensamples* (examples) (and types) *and they are written for our admonitions* (warnings) *upon whom the ends of the world* (ages) *are come."* We would do well to examine the examples in the Bible.

Moses and the Israelites are mentioned specifically in 1 Corinthians 10, and we will consider them later in this chapter. But, God established his way of dealing with people as "examples...for us."

Was Job raptured out of his time of tribulation (testing)? No! We know that in God's sight Job was *"...a perfect and upright* (righteous) *man, one that feareth* (reveres) *God and escheweth* (avoids) *evil,"* (Job 1:8). We find in Job 1:12 that God allowed Satan to start a time of tribulation for Job, but Satan was not given power to destroy (kill) Job; *"And the Lord said unto Satan, 'Behold, all that he hath is in thy power* (control)*; only upon himself put **not** forth thine hand.'''* Remember, God has promised us that He will *not* allow us to be tested beyond what we are able to endure (1 Cor. 10:13). This is reaffirmed in 1 Thessalonians 5:9, *"For God hath not appointed us to wrath, but to obtain salvation by our Lord Jesus Christ, Who died for us..."*

Another example for us would be Joseph (Gen. Chapters 37 through 46). Joseph was sold into slavery by his brothers, and was put in prison on false charges by the pharaoh's wife. From prison Joseph became identified as one who could hear from God, and after interpreting the pharaoh's dream, Joseph was "made ruler over all the land of Egypt." He was *not* raptured out of the pit his brothers put him in, nor his trip across the desert, nor his time in prison and he *was* rewarded *in* the world.

Consider Daniel in the lions' den (Dan. 6:7-28). Daniel was *not* raptured out of the lions' den, but the Lord saw him through the ordeal as an *overcomer.*

King David *overcame* much tribulation and was rewarded *in* the world. No rapture for King David!

The Israelites in Egypt are an outstanding example for *"us upon whom the end of the ages have come."* The Israelites were *in* Egypt for all ten plagues of God's wrath on the Egyptians, but the Israelites were kept safe and sound *right in the midst of it all as an example to the Egyptians* (and us) that God was with them (Exodus 7:18 through 12:30). The true Biblical believers will also be *overcomers,* witnesses (examples) to the unbelievers of the world as to the keeping power of our Lord during the time of great tribulation. If believers were raptured out of the world, there would be no such witness on the earth to draw multitudes to a saving knowledge of our Lord Jesus Christ. Revelation 12:11, *"And they* (Biblical believers) **overcame** *him* (Satan/Devil v. 9) *by the blood of the Lamb and by the word of their testimony* (witness)*, and they did not love* *their lives to the death.''* No rapture for the believers at the end of the age out of the plagues of God's wrath; rather *power* to witness at the risk of their lives! For God to remove his people during time of trouble at the end of the world (tribulation) would be completely against every example He gave us, including Jesus and the twelve disciples and the apostle Paul!

We find another outstanding example for end-time Biblical believers during the time of great tribulation in the *example* of the three Hebrew men during their time in Babylon under the rule of King Nebuchadnezzar. They are identified in Daniel 3:12-30 by their Babylonian names, Shadrach, Meshach and Abednego. (Their Hebrew names were: Hananiah, Mishael and Azariah, Dan. 1:19.)

They would *not* serve King Nebuchadnezzar's ''gods nor worship the golden image.'' The King gave them another chance to ''fall down and worship the golden image.'' If they did not, the King would have them ''cast into a burning fiery furnace seven times hotter than usual.'' The Hebrew men's response was, ''We are not sure what our God whom we serve will do, but *He is able to deliver us* from the fiery furnace and He will deliver us out of your hands, O King. We will *not* serve your gods and we will not worship the golden image you have made.'' When they did *not* ''fall down and worship the golden image,'' the King ''commanded the most mighty men of his army to bind Shadrach, Meshach and Abednego and cast them into the burning, fiery furnace…the exceeding hot furnace consumed (slew/destroyed) the men (soldiers).'' The King looked into the burning, fiery furnace and asked his counselors, ''Did not we cast *three men bound* into the middle of the fire?'' They answered, ''Yes, O King.'' Then the King said, ''Lo, I see *four men loose* (not bound), walking in the middle of the fire and they are not hurt; and the form of the *fourth man* is like the Son of God.''

When the three Hebrew men came out of the burning fiery

furnace, the King and *all* present saw that "fire had no power upon their bodies, nor was an hair on their heads singed, neither were their coats changed, nor the smell of fire upon them. Then Nebuchadnezzar said, 'Blessed be the God of Shadrach, Meshach and Abednego *in* Babylon.'"

Again, God is consistent, He kept/saved them from the fire *in* the furnace (*not* raptured out of it) before the eyes of those who would have destroyed them. They were a witness as to the overcoming power of God to all the unbelievers in Babylon and God prospered them *in* Babylon. The same was true of the Israelites, Joseph, Job, Daniel and David. And there are other examples.

But there is more to learn from the *example* of Shadrach, Meshach and Abednego. They would not worship any other god or golden image. In Revelation 13:8 we find that in these "last days" that *"ALL that dwell upon the earth shall worship him* (the beast) *whose names are not written in the Book of Life of the Lamb."* The three Hebrew men were overcomers—so must we be. God promises that *"He who overcomes will, like them be dressed in white* (righteousness). *I will never blot out his name from the Book of Life..."* (Revelation 3:5, NIV). They went *through* the burning fiery furnace for the Son of God was with them as in Psalm 23:4, *"Yea, though I walk **through** the valley of the shadow of death, I will fear no evil, for thou art with me..."* God has promised us, *"I will never leave thee, nor forsake thee,"* (Deut. 31:6, 8 and Heb. 13:5). God will be with you even *in* the time of the "great tribulation" to see you *through!*

We also find that the fire which destroyed (consumed) the *wicked* who threw them (the three Hebrews) into the furnace (just as the tares were destroyed by fire), was the *same fire* (tribulation - God's wrath) which set the Hebrew men (the wheat) *free!* God's Word confirms that this is God's way.

In Daniel 11:35 (Amplified Bible), *"And some of those*

30

who are wise, prudent and understanding shall be weakened and fall; (thus, then the *insincere* among the people will lose courage and become deserters). *It will be a test* (tribulation) *to refine, to purify and make those among* (God's people) *pure, even to the time of the end; because it is yet for a time* (God) *appointed''*—the time of the great tribulation?

Remember the promise that you shall *not* be tested/tempted *beyond* your (God given) strength/ability/power to endure (1 Cor. 10:13). Jesus also assured us that the ''great tribulation'' will be shortened in duration that the very elect might survive (Mat. 24:22).

We can also see a possible Biblical type in the ''burning fiery furnace that was *seven* times hotter than a normal fire.'' In Bible numerics, the number seven (7) speaks of, and is associated with, spiritual *perfection*. Could survival in this intense heat be a prophecy that the ''end-time'' Biblical believers can survive in a thermonuclear/atomic explosion? Isaiah 43:2, *''...when thou walkest **through** the fire, thou shalt **not** be burned; neither shall the flame kindle upon* (burn you).'' Psalm 91:7-8, *''A thousand shall fall at thy side and ten thousand at thy right hand; but it shall not come nigh thee* (near you). *Only with thine eyes shalt thou behold and see the reward* (destruction) *of the wicked.''* Just like the ''wheat and tares'' and ''As in the days of Noah.'' But, no rapture!

As clearly as the above Old Testament examples testify against a rapture doctrine, there is yet one other example that should leave *no* doubt—the life of our Lord Jesus Christ. He is the most significant single example to all Biblical believers as an example and pattern for us. In fact, His life would be the *primary* example we might expect to follow. Let us look at His life example/pattern on this earth because we are *''For whom he did foreknow, he also did predestinate to be conformed to the image of His Son,*

31

that He might be the firstborn among many brethren," (Rom. 8:29). 1 Peter 2:21 makes this even clearer, "For even hereunto were ye called, because Christ also suffered for us, leaving us an **example**, that ye should **FOLLOW** His steps (example/pattern)." And in 1 John 4:17, "...that we may have boldness in the day of judgment (tribulation); because as He (Jesus) is, so are we in this world."

We learn from Luke 4:1-14, "And Jesus, being full of the Holy Ghost (Spirit)...was led by the Spirit into the wilderness, being forty days tempted (tried, tested exceedingly) by the devil." notice, Jesus was *not* raptured out of this time of tribulation (pressure—affliction), but went *through* it by the power of God's Word and the Holy spirit as an overcomer. It was not until *after* this testing that "...Jesus returned in the power of the Holy Spirit" to begin His ministry *in* the world.

In Matthew 26:36 and Mark 14:32 we find our Lord Jesus Christ in a place called Gethsemane for yet another time of exceedingly severe testing or tribulation. Again, He was *not* raptured out of this tribulation, but came through it as an *overcomer*.

Matthew 27, Mark 15, Luke 23 and John 19 record the crucifixion of our Lord Jesus Christ. The purpose of His death (crucifixion) is revealed to us in John 3:16 and Romans 5:10; "...We were reconciled to God by the death of His Son." Again, Jesus, our *example*, was *not* raptured out of the trial, the mocking, the scourging, the struggle to Golgotha carrying the cross, being nailed to the cross, nor the six hours on the cross. Jesus went through it all as an *overcomer*, as an *example* for all Biblical believers. No rapture out of, or before His tribulations on earth!

The apostles followed the *example* of Jesus, not one was raptured out of his times of tribulation. For an example, look at St. Paul "...in prisons more frequent, in deaths oft. Of the Jews five times received I forty stripes (lashes) save

32

one. Thrice was I beaten with rods; once was I stoned (and left for dead)*; thrice I suffered shipwreck; a night and a day I have been in the deep* (sea)*; in journeyings often, in perils of waters, in perils of robbers, in perils by mine own countrymen* (the Romans)*; in perils of the heathen* (Gentiles)*, in perils in the city; in perils in the wilderness; in perils in the sea; in perils among false brethren; in weariness and painfulness, in watchings* (sleeplessness) *often, in hunger and thirst, in fastings often, in cold and nakedness,"* (2 Cor. 11:23-27). No rapture for St. Paul!

You can search the Scriptures, both Old and New Testaments, and you will *not* find anyone of God's chosen/elect being raptured out of their times of testing/tribulation!

In the Scriptures we find God often raised up armies to destroy His enemies. His army of these days is called the *"Overcomers"*. His past armies were *not* removed from the battle field—they were victorious. So shall His end-time army be! No rapture, but victory!

In Psalm 103:7 it is written, *"He* (God) *made known His ways to Moses, His acts unto the children of Israel."* The Scriptures make it repeatedly and abundantly clear that rapture is *not* God's way!

God has never taken (raptured) anyone of His out of their times of testings (tribulation) and He assures us He will not, *"For I am the Lord, I change not,"* (Malachi 3:6).

In Hebrews 3:10 we are told God *"was grieved* (not pleased) *with that* (wilderness, v.9) *generation, and said, 'They do always err in their heart and they have not known my ways.'"* You now know God's ways and can choose whether to continue in the rapture belief.

5

I Thessalonians 4:17

Now, as promised, we come to the one and *only* Scripture that even suggests the Biblical believers (saints, church, elect or body of Christ) will be removed (caught up) from the earth/world. However, the Scriptures charge us *not* to establish doctrines on one single Scripture. *"And for that the dream was doubled unto Pharaoh* **twice***; it is because the thing* **is** *established by* **God***, and God will shortly bring it to pass"* (Gen. 41:32). *"For God speaketh once, yea,* **twice***"* (Job 33:14). *"At the mouth of* **two** *witnesses, or* **three** *witnesses, shall he that is worthy of death be put to death; but at the mouth of* **one** *witness he shall not be put to death,"* (Deut. 17:6). *"In the mouth of* **two** *or* **three** *witnesses shall every word be established,"* (2 Cor. 13:1). Therefore, to establish a rapture doctrine on only one Scripture is a *most serious violation* of God's Holy Word!

Very few congregations, assemblies, or denominational

churches wash one another's feet before participating in Holy Communion as Jesus said we should and did by setting the *example* for us to follow in John 13:14, 15. *"If I* (Jesus) *then, your Lord and Master, have washed your feet, ye also ought to wash one another's feet. For I have given you an example, that you should do as I have done to you."*

Those who choose *not* to follow this clear command and example of our Lord Jesus Christ cite the fact that it only appears *once* in the Scriptures. Yet, some of these same congregations, assemblies, and denominations accept, proclaim and perpetuate a rapture doctrine based on *one single* verse of Scripture, 1 Thessalonians 4:17. The kindest thing that can be said about such a practice is that it is *inconsistent!*

To establish and maintain a rapture doctrine on the *one* "caught up" verse is a violation of the Bible principle that requires *"two or three"* and puts it in direct conflict with and *contradiction* to some fifty Scriptures, examples of Old Testament persons and the example of the life of our *Lord Jesus Christ* here on earth.

Therefore, something must be wrong, because Jesus said, *"...the scriptures cannot be broken"* (be in conflict or contradiction) John 10:35, and they will be fulfilled. If God's Word contained conflictions and contradictions, it would cause confusion and *"God is not the author* (originator) *of confusion"* 1 Cor. 14:33. *"God is not a man that He should lie,* (have conflicts and contradictions in His Word) *neither the son of man, that He should repent"* (change His mind/ways) Num. 23:19.

So, perhaps there is something wrong with the rapture understanding and interpretation of 1 Thessalonians 4:17. The answer could be in language translation from Greek to English. Remember, the word, rapture, does *not* appear in the text of *any* translation of the Bible, in *any* language. The use of "fabricated" words instead of Bible terms or words, severely hampers a *"search of the Scriptures to see if*

35

these things be true.''

In response to this, members of the rapture doctrine say it came from the Latin word, *rapio*. That may be true but it is **not** pertinent nor relevant because, as far as we can determine, 1 Thessalonians was first written in Greek, not Latin. However, it is a fact that the King James Version of the Bible was translated from the Roman Catholic Latin version of the Bible.

A Latin to English dictionary defines the Latin word, *rapio* as: to seize, to take by force, to become one, and is the root word for the English word, rape.

With the very helpful instruments for a detailed word study, we may use *Young's Analytical Concordance Of The Bible* and *Strong's Exhaustive Concordance Of The Bible*. Each of these volumes contain each word contained in the King James Version of the Bible, showing the book, chapter and verse in which the word appears, gives a brief meaning of the word and shows the Hebrew or Greek word. *Young's Concordance* is the simplest and easiest to use, but *Strong's Concordance* has some advantages in learning the meanings of various words.

Looking in *Young's* under the word, *caught*, on page 149, we cannot find 1 Thessalonians 4:17 listed. So, we look for the words, *up* (Greek: *ano*), *up to* (heos), *to rise up* (anatello) on page 1016—still no 1 Thessalonians 4:17. However, 1 Thessalonians 4:17 is listed under the words catch up (Greek: *harpazo*). In the back of *Young's* in the Greek Lexicon on page 72, we find that *harpazo* appears thirteen (13) times in the New Testament (KJV) and is translated six (6) different ways: catch, catch away, catch (caught) up, pluck and take by force.

Strong's, on page 176, word #726, agrees with *Young's* and points out that *harpazo* is derived from word #138, *haireomal*, translating into English: to take for oneself, to prefer or choose. This and ''take by force'' of *Young's* agree with the English translation of the Latin word, *rapio*, to seize, to take by force.

A look at how the word *harpazo* is used in the twelve other Scriptures may give us some additional understanding of the word's meaning.

1. Catch

John 10:12, *"...and the wolf **catcheth** (harpazo) them"* (the sheep).

2. Catch away

Matthew 13:19, ...then the wicked one comes *"...and **catcheth away** (harpazo) that* (the word) *which was sown in his heart."*

Acts 8:39, after Philip baptized the eunuch, *"...the Spirit of the Lord **caught away** (harpazo) Philip,"* to Azotus.

3. Caught up

2 Corinthians 12:2-4, St. Paul writes, *"I knew a man in Christ above fourteen years ago (whether in the body, I cannot tell; or whether out of the body, I cannot tell: God knoweth) such an one **caught up** (harpazo) to the third heaven. And I knew such a man (whether in the body, or out of the body, I cannot tell: God knoweth) how that he was **caught up** (harpazo) into paradise and heard unspeakable words, which it is not lawful for a man to utter."* The question of "whether (Paul) was in the body or out of the body (in the Spirit)" is resolved by St. John in Revelations 1:10 where he says, *"I was in the spirit on the Lord's day."* Also in Revelations 4:1, 2, *"After this I* (John) *looked, and, behold, a door was opened in heaven: and the first voice which I heard was as it were a trumpet talking with me; which said, 'Come up hither* (here), *and I will shew* (show) *thee things which must be hereafter.' And immediately I was **in the spirit**: and behold, a throne was set in heaven, and one sat on the throne."*

Revelations 12:5, *"And she* (a woman in heaven, verse

1) *brought forth a man child, who was to rule all nations with a rod of iron; and her child was* **caught up** *(harpazo) unto God and to His throne.''* In context starting at Revelation 11:14, 15, this occurs during *"the third woe"* and after *"the seventh angel sounded"* (the seventh trumpet), and is clearly taking place *in* heaven. So, her child was *not caught up* from the earth to heaven, but was, as the Scriptures says, *"up unto God and to His throne.''* Up to a higher level *in* Heaven.

In 2 Corinthians 12:2 St. Paul tells us a man (John) was *"caught up to the third heaven.''*

4. Pluck

John 10:28 and 29, Jesus says, *"And I give unto them eternal life; and they shall never perish, neither shall any man* **pluck** *(harpazo) them out of my hand. My Father which gave them Me, is greater than all; and no man is able to* **pluck** *(harpazo) them out of My Father's hand.''*

5. Pull

Jude 23, *"And others save with fear,* **pulling** *(harpazo) them out of the fire; hating even the garment spotted by the flesh.''*

6. Take by force

Matthew 11:12, *"And from the days of John the Baptist until now the Kingdom of Heaven suffereth violence, and the violent* **take it by force** *(harpazo).''*

John 6:15, *"When Jesus therefore perceived that they would come and* **take him by force** *(harpazo), to make Him a king, He departed again into a mountain Himself alone.''* (Jesus knew the people wanted to force an earthly kingdom on Him.)

Acts 23:10, *"...the chief captain...commanded the soldiers to go down to* **take him** (St. Paul) **by force** *(harpazo) from among them, and bring him into the castle.''* (The captain used force to save Paul from the Sanhedrin.)

Not one of these twelve (of 13) Scriptures containing

harpazo have anything to do with the physical removal of living people from the earth/world to heaven! (Remember, John was "in the spirit" when he saw heaven and even Paul couldn't state that John's physical body left the earth.)

Another key phrase for those of the rapture belief in the rapture chapter, 1 Thessalonians 4:17, is *"to meet the Lord in the air."*

According to Young's Concordance, page 24, the Greek word translated, air, in this verse is *aer* and is the same in Strong's Concordance as the word #109.

The Greek word, *aer* (air), is used in the following Scriptures: Acts 22:23, *"...and threw dust into the air (aer)."* 1 Corinthians 9:26, *"...not as one who beateth the air (aer)."* And 1 Corinthians 14:9, *"...for ye shall speak into the air* (aer).*"*

There is another Greek word which is also translated, air, in the King James Version of the Bible. It is *ouranos* and appears in the following Scriptures: Matthew 6:26, 8:20, 13:32; Mark 4:4 & 32; Luke 8:5, 9:58, 13:19 and Acts 10:12, 11:6. Each one of these Scriptures refer to "the birds/fowls of the air *(ouranos)*."

So, we see if there was to be a rapture the peoples heads would go no higher than about ten feet above the earth's surface—no higher that you can "throw dust into the air *(aer)*." There is no way one can honestly make the word, *aer*, become "Heaven." We *are "in the air (aer)" now* with our feet on the ground (earth) and so shall we *"remain"* (v 15, 17)!

The rapture promoter makes much of Noah being lifted up above the earth by the flood waters as a type of rapture. Please notice that Noah was *not* lifted up to heaven, but *did remain "in the air (aer)!"*

There is another word that requires investigation to determine its meaning in this context *"with them* (the resurrected saints) *in the clouds."* In the following Scriptures, the divine *cloud* came *down to earth*; Matthew 17:5, Mark 9:7 and Luke 9:34. When Jesus was transfigured, *"a cloud came down* (they were on a mountain), *overshadowed them and behold, a voice out of the cloud which said, 'This is My beloved Son, in whom I am well pleased; hear ye Him.'"*

1 Corinthians 10:1,2, *"Moreover, brethren, I would not that ye be ignorant, how that all our fathers were under the cloud, and all passed through the sea; And were all baptized unto Moses in the cloud* (must have come down) *and in the sea."* But, the most appropriate for the 1 Thessalonians 4:17 *"cloud,"* is Hebrews 11:36 through 12:2: *"And others* (persons of the Old Testament— examples) *had trials of cruel mockings and scourgings, yea, moreover of bonds and imprisonment: They were stoned, they were sawn asunder, were tempted, were slain with the sword; they wandered about in sheepskins and goatskins; being destitute, afflicted, tormented; (Of whom the world was not worthy:) they wandered in deserts, and in mountains, and in dens and caves of the earth. And these all, having obtained a good report through faith, received not the promise: God having pro- vided* (foreseen) *some better thing for us, that they without us should not be made perfect. Wherefore, seeing we also are compassed about with so great a cloud of witnesses* (the spirits of the departed saints), *let us lay aside every weight, and the sin which does so easily beset us, and let us run with patience the race that is set before us, looking unto Jesus the author* (beginner) *and finisher of our faith."* And in Hebrews 6:1, we are exorted to *"go on unto perfection."*

In 1 Thessalonians 4:17 this "great cloud of witnesses" are at long last (in Rev. 6:10 we find the spirits of these departed saints crying, *"How long, O Lord..."*) having their spirits returned to the earth with Jesus (v 15) to be united with their resurrected bodies (v 16) to *"be made perfect"* with those *"who are alive and remain"* on the earth (v 15, 17), all this taking place at Christ's second coming.

Now, let us read 1 Thessalonians 4, beginning at verse 13, with a much more accurate and clearer understanding of the words and terms used therein. For clarity, the following Scripture quotes from 1 Thessalonians are in the bolder print. ***"But I would not have you ignorant, brethren, concerning them which are asleep*** (this Scripture is primarily about the departed/dead saints in Christ) ***that ye sorrow not, even as others which have no hope*** (the Sadducees did not believe in a resurrection). ***For if we believe that Jesus died and rose again*** (we all believe that)***, even so*** (in like manner) ***them also which sleep*** (are dead) ***in Jesus will God bring with Him*** (Jesus). ***For this we say unto you by the word of the Lord, that we*** (Biblical believers) ***who are alive and remain*** (on earth) ***unto the coming of the Lord shall not prevent*** (precede) (have any advantage over) ***them which are asleep. For the Lord Himself shall descend from heaven*** (Acts 1:11, Jesus went *directly* from earth to heaven and shall return "in like manner" *directly* from heaven to earth. *No* rapture back to heaven for a later *third coming!*) ***with a shout, with the voice of the archangel, and the trump***(et) ***of God: And the dead in Christ shall rise*** (Greek word, *anistemi*: to set up or be resurrected) ***first: Then we who are alive*** ("We shall not all die, but shall be changed/transformed/transfigured" (1 Cor 15:51) ***and remain*** (on the earth *in* the *"aer"*) ***shall be caught up*** (made one) *(harpazo)* ***together*** (at the same time) ***with them*** (the dead in Christ) ***in the clouds to meet the Lord in the air*** (the "great cloud of witnesses" that will "be made perfect" with us *on* earth when Jesus brings their *spirits* "with Him" to be united with their bodies resurrected out of the ground "first" into the air [aer] with us in the air, *on* the surface of the earth)***: and so shall we*** (for)***ever be with***

41

the Lord, (in the air [*aer*] here *on* earth forever)**. Wherefore, comfort** (reassure) **one another with these words.''** (Notice, the Lord "descended from heaven" before we are "caught up" to him; just as the "New Jerusalem" came down to dwell with us—Rev. 21:2.)

To choose to translate the word, *harpazo,* to the English phrase, *"made one"* in verse 17 is as accurate an option as any of the six other ways it is translated in the King James Version of the Bible. This *"made one"* removes 1 Thessalonians 4:17 as a contradiction to and in conflict with the many other Scriptures and Biblical examples. This would make 1 Thessalonians 4:17 the answer to the *prayer* of our Lord Jesus Christ (which will be fulfilled) in John 17:21-23, **"That they all may be** (made) **one, as thou, Father, art in Me, and I in Thee, that they also may be** (made) **one in us; that the world** (not heaven) **may believe that Thou hast sent Me. And the glory which Thou gavest Me I have given them; that they may be one, even as we are one: I in them, and Thou in Me, that they may be made perfect in one; and that the world may know that thou hast sent me, and hast loved them, as Thou hast loved Me.''**

While discussing the various translations of the Greek word, *harpazo* with a Christian brother of German origin, he checked 1 Thessalonians in his Bible, which was translated into German by Martin Luther. He said it was translated into a German word which could mean, "the lesser was included into the greater.'' We Christians are the "lesser'' and Jesus is the "Greater.'' This Martin Luther translation comes close to *"shall be made one.''* In John 10:12 *"...and the wolf 'harpazo' the sheep,''* the wolf ate the sheep and they were "made one'' or "the lesser was included into the greater.'' The same is true in Matthew 13:4 and 19 in Jesus' parable of the sowing of the *"seed''* which is the *"word of the kingdom''* where *"the fowls came and devoured the seeds,"* that is, "the wicked one *'harpazo'* that which is sown..." the fowls devoured/ate/consumed the seed/word. They were "made one" or "the lesser was included in the greater." It seems clear that Martin Luther did *not* see *"harpazo"* as being "caught up."

Jesus, our example, was changed/transformed/transfigured (Greek: metamorphoo) in the air *(aer)* standing right here on the surface on the earth. In exactly the same way *"we who are alive and remain* (on the earth) *shall also be"* changed/transfigured/transformed right here on the earth. 1 Corinthians 15:51-54, *"Behold, I shew you a mystery* (secret)*; We shall not all sleep* (die)*, but we shall all be changed in a moment, in the twinkling* (blinking) *of an eye, at the last trump*(et)*: for the trumpet shall sound, and the dead* (in Christ) *shall be raised incorruptible, and we shall be changed* (and made one with them)*. For this corruptible must put on incorruption, and this mortal must put on immortality. So when this corruptible shall have put on incorruption, and this mortal shall have put on immortality, then shall be brought to pass the saying that is written, 'Death is swallowed up in victory.'"* (1 Thes. 4:16, 17; Isa. 25:8) Also in 1 John 3:2 and Colossians 3:4, *"...it doth not yet appear what we shall be: but we know that when He* (Jesus) *shall appear, we shall be like Him."* Again it is so very clear that this all occurs right here on the surface of the earth in the air *(aer)*. John 14:23, Jesus says, *"If a man love Me, he will keep my words: and my Father will love him, and We will come unto him* (not bring us to him) *and make our abode with*(in) *him* (on the earth)*."* No mention of going to heaven in a rapture. Indeed, the 21st chapter of Revelations describes the new heaven and earth, with New Jerusalem coming *down* from heaven for God to dwell there with his people, Rev. 21:1, 2, 3, *"And I saw a new heaven and a new earth:*

for the first heaven and the first earth were passed away: and there was no more sea. And I John saw the Holy City, New Jerusalem coming down from God out of heaven, prepared as a bride adorned for her husband. And I heard a great voice out of heaven saying, 'Behold the tabernacle of God is with men, and He will dwell (down in New Jerusalem) *with them...'"*

In passing, it is interesting to note there was a resurrection of saints in Matthew 27:52, after His (Jesus') resurrection *"...the graves* (of the dead) *were opened; and many bodies of the saints which slept arose and came out of the graves after His resurrection and went into the holy city and appeared unto many."* (Notice, they were not seen streaking through the sky enroute to heaven singing, "I'll fly away, O glory!")

Some other points worth considering in 1 Thessalonians 4:17, 18 are that we will *"meet the Lord in the air* (here on the surface of the earth)*: and so* (in that exact manner; in the air and *on* the earth—*not* in heaven) *shall we* (for)*ever be with the Lord,"* (in the New Jerusalem where God will dwell with us). Notice it is *"forever"* that we shall be with the Lord in the air on the surface of the earth and *not* in heaven for seven or three and one-half years to return with Jesus in a *third* "coming."

(Can you imagine the raptured Christians in an aircraft type holding-pattern about ten feet above the earth's surface in the air *(aer)* for seven or three and one half years to return (short trip) to the earth?!)

Many Biblical believers and well-known radio and television evangelists, pastors and teachers do not know the difference between their spirit and soul, and erroneously use the words synonymously and interchangeably. Therefore, their understanding of Bible Truth is limited and flawed.

1 Thessalonians 5:23 says, *"And the very God of*

peace sanctify you wholly (completely)*; and I pray God your whole spirit* (Greek: Pneuma)*, and soul* (Greek: Psyche) *and body* (Greek: Soma) *be preserved blameless unto the coming of the Lord Jesus Christ.*" Briefly, you are a *spirit* and it is God-given. You have a *soul* which is your mind, will, intellect and emotions. Your *spirit* and your *soul* are residing in a body. How else can we understand what St. Paul is teaching us in 2 Corinthians 1:10, *"... God which raiseth the dead: Who delivered us* (past tense; spirit) *from so great a death, and Who doth deliver* (present, ongoing tense: soul)*: in whom we trust that He will yet deliver us* (future tense: body)*.*" Or when St. Paul says in 2 Corinthians 5:6, 8, *"...while we* (spirits) *are at home in the body, we are absent from the Lord...I say, and willing rather to be absent* (spiritually) *from the body, and to be present with the Lord.*" These and other Scriptures explain that upon the death of a Biblical believer, the spirit returns to the Lord. Therefore, we understand it is their *spirits* the Lord Jesus Christ *"will bring with Him"* when He *returns,* (1 Thes. 4:14).

Jesus refers to this event in John 5:28, *"Do not be amazed at this, for a time is coming in which all who are in their graves will hear His voice and come out..."* (NIV).

The word, "redemption," in the Bible is most often related to the body (soma) as in Romans 8:23, *"...ourselves also, which have the firstfruits of the Spirit, even we ourselves groan within ourselves, waiting for the adoption...the redemption of our body."*

Now we can understand the meaning of Luke 21:28, NIV, where Jesus says, *"When these things begin to take place* (signs of the "end of the age")*, stand up and lift your heads* (do not be sad or depressed)*, because your redemption is drawing near."* That is your transformation, and the resurrection may be very near as per 1 Corinthians 15:51 and 1 Thessalonians 4:17.

By now we could say, "the rapture has been *canceled*, due to lack of supporting Scriptures!"

6

"Rapture" Support Arguments

Christians who believe the rapture doctrine use considerable inductive and deductive reasonings to support this doctrine, through implied means they believe they can attribute to Scriptures. We shall explore some of their favorites.

They attribute much importance to the *fact* that the word, *church,* does not appear after chapter four of the Book of Revelation (Rev. 4). Therefore, they deduce/conclude that the *church* must have been raptured out of the world, up to heaven. To accept this idea, they have to ignore Ephesians 4:11-12 and 5:27 which tell us *"And He* (Jesus) *gave some,* (to be) *apostles; and some, prophets; and some, evangelists; and some, pastors and teachers; for the perfecting* (equipping) *of the saints for the work of ministry, for the edifying of the Body of Christ...that He* (Jesus) *might present it to Himself a glorious church..."* These verses and others make it so very clear that the terms: *saints, Body of Christ* and *church* are the *same people* and are synonymous terms. *Saints* are mentioned thirteen (13) times *after* Revelation 4 and are clearly *still on earth*. They are: Revelation 5:8, *"...which are the prayers of the Saints."* 8:3, 4, *"...offer(ing) it with the prayers of all the saints upon the golden altar which was before the throne. And the smoke of the incense, which came with the prayers of the saints."* 11:18, *"...that Thou* (God) *shouldest give reward unto thy servants the prophets, and to the saints."* 13:7, *"And it was given unto him* (the beast, v.4) *to make war with the saints."* Notice, the *saints/church/Body of Christ* are *on* the earth during the time of the Antichrist, (Mr. 666). This is contrary to the doctrine of rapture. Revelations 13:10, *"...Here is the patience and faith of the saints."* 14:12, *"Here is the patience of the saints: here are they that keep the commandments of God, and the faith of Jesus."* 15:3 *"...Thou King of the saints."* 16:6, *"For they have shed the blood of the saints and prophets..."* 17:6, *"I saw the woman drunken with the blood of the saints..."* 18:24, *"And in her was found the blood of prophets and the saints, and of all that were slain upon the earth."* 19:8, *"And to her* (the bride of the Lamb, v.7) *was granted that she should be arrayed in fine linen, clean and white: for the fine linen is the righteousness of the saints."* 20:9, *"And they* (Gog and Magog, v.8) *went up on the breadth of the earth, and compassed the camp of the saints about, and the beloved city: and fire came down from God out of heaven, and devoured them* (Gog and Magog).*"* Again, the *saints/church/Body of Christ* are still here on earth for this display of God's power. No rapture, but kept safe in it! Revelation 13:7 tells us the *"beast makes war against the saints,"* but the rapture believers have the *saints* raptured out of the world before the beast and his worldwide system is established. Therefore, they are seldom interested in the fact that a worldwide, one world government and one

48

world economic system may well be functioning now (1989), and that we may be very close to a system of "buying and selling" with an identification mark/number in/on the "right hand or forehead," as prophesied in Revelation 13:16-17. How sad! Maybe this book will awaken them, before it is too late and the bridegroom has come, but some were not ready: *"Behold, the bridegroom cometh, go ye **out** (not up!) to meet him,"* (Matt. 25:6).

Some rapture promoters contend that the *saints* mentioned after chapter four are 144,000 Jewish evangelists. They have not even *one* Scripture to support this contention. The list of the twelve Hebrew tribes in Revelation 7:4-8 shows only *"12,000 of the tribe of Judah,"* not 144,000. How could these evangelists come to the saving knowledge of the grace of the Lord Jesus Christ if *ALL* the true Biblical believers are raptured out of the world? Romans 10:13, 14, *"For whosoever shall call upon the name of the Lord shall be saved. How then shall they call upon Him in whom they have not believed? And how shall they believe in Him of whom they have not heard? How can they hear without a preacher?"* An interesting question.

The rapture teachers would have all in the world saved by 144,000, or 12,000 Jewish evangelists in seven years (pre-trib); or three and one-half years (mid-trib), when hundreds of millions of dedicated Biblical believers and evangelists have *not* been able to do it in nearly two thousand years! *"There is neither Greek* (Gentile) *nor Jew...but Christ is all and in all. Put on therefore, as the elect of God. . ."* (Col. 3:11-12). Paul clearly stated here that there was *no longer a distinction* between *Jew or Gentile*, we are all in Christ, the elect of God!

In addition, the book of Revelation clearly states that the *saints* are *in* the great tribulation (Rev. 7:13, 14): *"And one of the elders answered, saying unto me, 'What* (who) *are these which are arrayed in white robes? and whence*

49

came they?' And I said unto him, 'Sir, thou knowest,' And he said unto me, 'These are they which came out of the **great tribulation**, and have washed their robes, and made them white in the blood of the Lamb.'" There is good news for the *saints*. The prayer the Lord taught us to pray, in Matthew 6:10, Luke 11:2, *"...Thy Kingdom come. Thy will be done **on earth** as it is in heaven..."* is at last fulfilled. Revelation 11:15, *"The Kingdoms of this world have become **the Kingdom** of our Lord, and of His Christ."* Revelation 5:10, *"and we* (saints) *shall reign **on the earth**."* Revelation 20:4, (Those) *"which had not worshiped the beast, neither his image, neither had received his mark upon their foreheads or in* (on) *their hands; and they lived and reigned* (on earth) *with Christ a thousand years."* Only believers who are *on earth* at the time of the beast and the tribulation could have made *a choice* of whether or not to receive the mark of the beast, and it is quite clear in this passage, that those saints who lived (and some were killed, Rev. 6:9-11) during this end of times, are those who are rewarded by reigning on earth with Christ for the thousand years. *"But the **rest of the dead lived not again until the thousand years were finished. This is** the first resurrection,"* (Rev. 20:5).

The *saints* get a total victory in Revelation 15:2: *"and them* (saints) *that had gotten the **victory** over the beast, over his image and over his mark and over the number of his name..."* Revelation 12:11, *"And they **overcame** him* (the beast) *by the blood of the Lamb and the word of their testimony..."*

The tribulation *saints* are *overcomers, not copper-outers*! To teach overcoming and rapture is a contradiction! Rapture is the opposite of overcoming—it means "to escape."

The rapture believers insist that God would not pour out His wrath on the righteous of the world, therefore, (deductive reasoning) God must rapture them out of the world before

50

the "beast" (an agent of the devil's power) takes over. They are inadvertently saying that the devil is more powerful than God! God *can* keep us from the evil one!

The Scripture they most often quote is 1 Thessalonians 5:9, *"God did not appoint us* (saints) *to wrath, but to obtain salvation through our Lord Jesus Christ."* This is a beautiful Scripture, and interestingly enough, the word, *obtain*, is defined thus: *obtain*—to get possession of by *trying*; procure—vi. to *prevail*—to be *victorious*! *Victorious*—having *won* a victory! This means "to *obtain* salvation," we do *not* "get possession of" by *escaping*, and we *cannot* be *victorious* by "having *escaped* a victory!" We must *try* and win!

As God's elect (saints), we can obtain *all* His promises, which assure us He will see us through *all* that shall come upon the earth in the time of the "great tribulation." These Scriptures were given in Chapter 3 of this book.

It is difficult to determine the difference between the "wrath of God," which destroys the wicked, and "tribulation," which perfects the saints. It is doubtful one could have convinced the people of Egypt that the ten plagues which came upon them were *not* the "wrath of God." However, the Israelites were kept *in* it and seen *through* it.

If you will read in Exodus, chapter 12, verses 21 to 29, Moses instructs the Israelites to take a hyssop branch and *dip it in the blood of a sacrificed lamb* and *"mark"* their doorposts with this blood, so that the destroying angel of the Lord will *not harm them.* Then in Revelations, chapter 7, we read that whoever is alive at the time of tribulation will receive a "seal/mark" of God before He releases his angels to destroy and hurt. Rev. 7:3,4: *"Saying, 'Hurt not the earth, neither the sea, nor the trees, till we have **sealed the servants of our God in their foreheads.'** And I heard the number of them which were sealed: and there were sealed an hundred and forty and four thousand of all the tribes of the children of Israel."*

This is the passage (Rev. 7:4) that has led some to suppose that only 144,000 *Jews* will be on earth at this time; and the Jehovah's Witnesses believe that only those of their members who *know they are one of the 144,000 chosen ones can receive communion on this earth, and they must earn* that right.

However, though no earthly man can state exactly *who* those 144,000 are, keep in mind *two* things: 1) when God ordered a count, women and children were *not* included in the total, thus there may be **many more** than 144,000, and 2) Rev. 14:4 says, *". . . These were the redeemed from among men, being the firstfruits unto God and the Lamb."*

The Bible tells us much about *firstfruits*. They are the *top* and *best portion* that we give the Lord, but *not* the *largest portion*! Perhaps, as shown *throughout* the old and new testaments, God chose certain men to *show the way* and suffer and be martyrs, such as Stephen. One thing *is* certain, whoever they (144,000) may be, they did *not* suffer the *wrath/plagues* God sent—the *seal* of God spared them!

Remember what happened to the soldiers who threw the three Hebrew men into the burning fiery furnace—the *same* fire (wrath of God) that destroyed the soldiers (wicked) set the Hebrew men (God's chosen) free! So shall it be!

The Book of Revelation contains many symbolisms and symbolic numbers, like 666 in Revelation 13:18. The number six (6) relates to Adamic or unredeemed man. Likewise the New Jerusalem of Revelation 21 is multiples of the number twelve (12). Twelve is associated with and represents God's divine order. The number one-thousand (1,000) may represent and indicate multitudes or an infinitely large number. Therefore, the 144,000 (12 x 12 x 1,0000) may be referring to multitudes living in God's divine order. The *"manifested sons of God"*!

In Revelation 21:2, we find *"the New Jerusalem* (a

52

type/representation of God's divine order) (is) *coming **down out of heaven***" to earth and mankind…remember our constant prayer: When *"Thy Kingdom had come, Thy* (purpose/objective) *will* (have been) *done **on** earth as it is **now** in heaven."* Just when this prayer is being answered/fulfilled, the rapture believer would be going up and would miss it!

Another of their favorites is John 14:2, 3 where Jesus says, *"In My Father's house are many mansions; if it were not so, I would have told you. And if I go and prepare a place for you, **I will come again** and receive you unto Myself; that where I am, there you may be also."* Jesus said, *"I will come again," not,* "you will come up to me."

One of the factors which confuses our understanding of these two verses are the Greek words translated, *House* and *mansion*. *The Greek word translated, house,* is *oikia,* and is used 111 times and is translated *five* different ways: home (5), house (102), household or family (3) and temple (1). *Strong's Concordance*, word #3614/3624, "residence; an abode, family and dwelling."

The Greek word translated, *mansions* is *mone* and is used 119 times and is translated *fourteen* different ways. It is translated *mansion* only one time! By far the most consistent translation is *"abide/abode,"* sixty times. *Strong's Concordance*, word #3438/3306, "a staying/enduring residence or abode." This Greek word, *mone* appears five times in this chapter and is translated *mansion* in verse 2, *dwelling* twice in verses 10 and 17, *abode* in verse 23. This lack of consistence in the King James Version is confusing.

Also in the phrase *"…that where I am, **there** you may be also,"* the word, *there,* is italicized because it is *not* in the original Greek text. In other words, the *there* is *not* there!

A more accurate, consistent and understandable translation might read as follows: "In my Father's *abode* there are many enduring (permanent) *abodes*; if it were not so, I would have told you. And if I *go* and prepare a place for you, I will *come* again, and receive you *into* Myself; that where *I am* you may be also.''

In the context of this chapter and other Scriptures, we can understand what the Lord Jesus Christ is telling us. ''In My Father's *dwelling place* there are many *dwelling places* (verses 17, 20); if it were not so, I would have told you. I *go* to prepare a (dwelling) place for you (among My Father's many *dwelling places*). (After I have prepared a place for you) I will *come* again,'' (verse 23), *''We* (My Father and I) *will come unto him and make our abode with him* (dwelling place)'' Notice, They *come* to us. We do *not* go to Them. Also, John 17:21-24 Jesus prays, *''That they all may be one; as thou, Father, are in Me, and I in You, that they also may be one in us: that the world may believe that Thou have sent Me. And the glory which Thou gavest Me I have given them; that they may be one, even as We are one: I in them, and Thou in Me, that they may be made perfect in one; and that the world may believe that Thou hast sent Me, and have loved them, as Thou hast loved Me...that they also, whom Thou hast given me, be with me where I am.''* (Physically, Jesus was standing *on the earth*. Spiritually, He and His Father were *one*, just as Jesus prayed we shall also be one, here on earth.)

Indeed, Jesus spoke a blessing in John 16:7, *''It is expe-dient* (better) *for you that I go away...''* Remember, *''Christ in you the hope of glory''* (Colossians 1:27). And *''He* (Jesus) *shall come to be glorified in His saints* (here on earth).''* Also, 1 Corinthians 12:13, *''For by one Spirit are we all* (you) *baptized into one body,* (dwelling place).''*

Some try to promote their rapture belief by quoting Luke 21:36, *''...pray always, that you may be accounted wor-thy to escape all these things that shall come to pass and to stand before the Son of Man.''* The key word, *worthy* is translated from the Greek word, *axios,* and means

54

"deserving or merit". We find in Revelation 3:4, 5, that *only* the *overcomers* are *worthy* to *"be clothed in white raiment* (righteousness).*"* How do we overcome? Revelation 12:11, *"And they **overcame** him* (Satan/Devil) *by the blood of the Lamb and by the **word of their testimony*** (living witness)*; and they* (the overcomers) *loved not their lives unto death."* Revelation 5:2-9 tells us that *"...no man in heaven, nor in the earth, neither under the earth, was able* (worthy) *to open the book, neither to look there on."* Jesus *was* worthy, but He did *not escape* His tribulations here on earth: during His forty days and nights in the wilderness being tested by the Devil/Satan himself (Luke 4:1-13); in the Garden of Gethsemane sweating blood (Luke 22:42-44); and His crucifixion (Matthew 27, Mark 15, Luke 23 and John 19).

Can you imagine any greater tribulations than those of Jesus? Remember, He is our prime example/pattern! Also, He (Jesus) *comes to us* (John 14:3, 18, 23) we do *not go* to Him that we might *"stand before the Son of Man* (here on earth).*"*

It is also well to note that some other more recent translations of the Bible (New American Standard, New English, J.B. Phillips' New Testament In Modern English, Ratherham's Emphasized Bible, New International Version, Jerusalem Bible, Good News Bible, Ferrar Fenton's Bible In Modern English, et al) do *not* use the words *"be accounted worthy to escape"* as in the King James Version. Most translations of the Bible agree with the Jerusalem Bible which translates Luke 21:36 this way, *"Stay awake, praying at all times for the strength to survive all that is going to happen, and stand with confidence before the Son of Man."* Yes, the overcomers *go through*, they do *not* fly away!

Some of the rapture's favorite teachers, annotated Bibles and commentaries make much of Enoch and Elijah, who did not see death, to say that they are a type of the church being taken from the earth in a rapture. But, Jesus said ever so plainly and clearly that, *"at the coming of the Son of Man it would be as in the days of Noah"* (Matthew 24:37 and Luke 17:26). *not "as in the days of Enoch and Elijah!" Also, Enoch and Elijah were not* removed because *some tribulation* was upon them, rather, God chose to end their lives on earth in this manner.

Another favorite of the rapture promoters is 2 Thessalonians 2:5-8, *"Do you not remember that when I was still with you, I told you these things? And you know what is restraining, that he may be revealed in his own time. For the mystery of lawless is already at work; only he who now restrains will do so until he is taken out of the way,"* (New King James). The "escapist" contends that *"he who now restrains* (K.J.V.: *"letteth")* *will do so* (will let) *until he is taken out of the way,"* refers to the Holy Spirit and /or the church/saints/body of Christ/ Christians who are restraining evil and will do so until they are "taken out of the way" in a rapture.

This can *not* be true because no one could be saved during the "great tribulation" without the Holy Spirit who "convicts" mankind of their sin (see John 16:8): *"And when He* (Holy Spirit, 'Comforter' v. 7) *is come, He will* (convict/convince/reprove) *the world of sin."* Neither can this Scripture be referring to the church. Remember Romans 10:14: *"How then shall they* (the unsaved) *call upon Him in whom they have not believed? And how shall they believe in Him of whom they have not heard? And how shall they hear without a preacher?"* Therefore, the Christians cannot depart in a rapture!

The clearest and most complete explanation and understanding of what 2 Thessalonians 2:1-8 is telling us, that I have read, is contained in a book, *"Great Prophecies Of The Bible"* **by Ralph Woodrow, P.O. Box 124, Riverside,**

CA 92592 and, with the author's permission, is quoted as follows:

"HE WHO LETTETH WILL LET"

*"Now we beseech you, brethren, by the coming of our Lord Jesus Christ, and by our gathering together unto him...Let no man deceive you by any means: for that day shall not come, except there come a **falling away first**, and that **man of sin be revealed**...and now ye know what witholdeth that he might be revealed in his time...only he who now letteth will let, until he be taken out of the way. And then shall that **Wicked** be revealed"* (2 Thess. 2:1-8).

"Has the man of sin been revealed yet? During World War I, some believed the Kaiser would be the dreaded man of sin, the Antichrist. A few years later it was Joseph Stalin. When the New Deal came into power in the United States, some thought Franklin Roosevelt was at least the forerunner of Antichrist. And then, of course, there was Mussolini and Hitler. Of the two, Mussolini was probably the favorite. A book published in 1940 asked the question: *'Is Mussolini the Antichrist?'* and the writer answered: 'He may be. I know of no reason why he should not fit the description of the terrible man of sin...He is evidently an atheist.' (1) Another writer was more positive in his claims. He said that Mussolini had fulfilled 49 prophecies concerning Antichrist!

"Actually, it would take several pages to give an account of the various ideas that are held today concerning Antichrist. But the common concept is that he will be an atheistic 'superman,' an individual who will come to worldwide political power and prominence during the last years of this age. This is the futurist interpretation.

"In contrast to the futurist interpretation is what we will call the fulfilled interpretation. Those who hold this view believe the prophecies concerning the man of sin, or

Antichrist, have found their fulfillment in the papacy...the succession of Popes who rose to power in Rome following the fall of the Roman Empire. To some, this interpretation will appear too ridiculous to even consider, and it will be cast aside immediately. But before such actions are taken, surely the evidence for this position should be carefully examined. As we shall note in more detail later, such well-known men as **Wyclif, Huss, Luther, Calvin Knox, Zwingli, Tyndale, Foxe, Newton and Wesley**, all believed that the prophecies of the man of sin had found their fulfillment in the Roman Papacy. Should we not at least inquire why these men held this view?

"Looking again now at Paul's prophecy regarding the man of sin, we read these words: *'Remember ye not, that, when I was yet with you, I told you these things? And now ye know what witholdeth that he* (the man of sin) *might be revealed in his time. For the mystery of iniquity doth already work: only he who now letteth* (restrain), *until he be taken out of the way. And then shall that Wicked be revealed,'* (2 Thess. 2:5-8). The word, 'let' in this passage is simply an old English word meaning, 'to hinder or restrain.' In this case, the reference is to something that was hindering or restraining the appearance of the man of sin.

"We notice from the wording of this passage that whatever was restraining the man of sin from being revealed was not something unknown or obscure. Paul knew what it was. He mentioned the Christians at Thessalonica knew what it was. There was no guess work about it. However, when writing concerning this restraint, we notice that Paul was careful not to mention it by name, but simply reminded them of what he taught when he had been present with them.

"What was it that was restraining or hindering the man of sin from being revealed? According to the teachings handed down by word of mouth to the Christians of the early centuries, it was the Roman Empire under the Caesars, the fall of which would bring on the man of sin.

"**Justin Martyr** in his **Apologies** to the pagan Roman rulers, stated that the Christians' understanding of the time caused them to pray for the continuance of the restraining Roman Empire, lest the dreaded times of Antichrist, expected to follow upon its fall, should overtake them in their day. (6)

"**Chrysostom** stated: 'One may naturally inquire, What is that which witholdeth?' He answered that it was the Roman Empire, 'when the Roman Empire is taken out of the way, then he (Antichrist) shall come. And naturally. For as long as the fear of this empire lasts, no one will willingly exalt himself, but when that is dissolved, he will attack the anarchy, and endeavor to seize upon the government both of man and God.' He spoke also of how the four empires of Daniel 7 each followed the others in succession, so the fall of Rome would be followed by Antichrist. 'As Rome succeeded Greece, so Antichrist is to succeed Rome.' (14)

"**The Encyclopedia Britannica** says the power which was universally believed by the Christians to be that which was retarding the revelation of the Antichrist was the Roman Empire. (19)

"**Clarke's Commentary** states the united testimony of the church leaders of those first centuries was that the restraint which was to be removed was the Roman Empire. (20)

"Understanding that it was the Roman Empire to be removed before the man of sin would come to power, we can now understand why Paul did not come right out and call the hindrance by name. To teach 'eternal Rome' could fall from power, could have brought the early Christians into immediate conflict with the leaders and people of the Empire within which they lived. Especially careful would Paul be in writing to the Christians at Thessalonica, for

59

when he had been there with them, unbelieving Jews had stirred up trouble by saying that Christians were doing things 'contrary to the decrees of Caesar' and that they believed in *another king, one Jesus,'* (Acts 17:7). So, when writing to the Thessalonian believers, he found it wise to simply remind them of what he had taught when he had been present with them.

"***Jerome*** said Paul believed the restraint was the Roman Empire, and that 'if he had chosen to say this openly, he would have foolishly aroused a frenzy of persecution against the Christians.'" (22) Chrysostom stated: 'Because he (Paul) said this of the Roman Empire, he naturally glanced at it, and speaks covertly and darkly, for he did not wish to bring upon himself (and others) superfluous enmities, and useless dangers.' (23)

"Understanding the 'let' or restraint standing in the way was the Roman Empire, and its fall would bring on the man of sin, we can now know the time when the man of sin rose to power! We should look not to the future for the appearance of the man of sin then, but back into those early centuries to the time of the fall of the Roman Empire.

"Looking again at Paul's prophecy (2 Thess. 2), we notice included within his veiled description is not only the mention of 'what' witholdeth, but also 'he' who letteth or restrains (verses 6, 7). *'What,'* is neuter gender; *'he,'* is masculine. Evidently, the reference was to the Roman Empire as, *'what'* and to Caesar as, *'he'* who would be taken out of the way.

"If, then, Caesar would have to be 'taken out of the way' before the man of sin could come to power, we have a strong indication that the man of sin would rise to power in Rome. It could not properly be said that Caesar was in the way of the man of sin, unless the Caesar was occupying the place the man of sin would eventually occupy!

"To illustrate, let us suppose we wanted to build a house on a certain piece of property, but another building was in the way. Obviously, it could not be said the old building was in the way and needed to be taken out of the way...unless it was occupying the spot where the new house would be built. The old building would not have to be taken out of the way if the new house was going to be built on a completely different location!

"Likewise, the Roman Caesar could not be in the way...and need to be 'taken out of the way'—unless the place he occupied would be the location where the man on sin would come to power! Therefore, since we have seen that the Roman Caesar was the 'he' that was in the way and would have to be 'taken out of the way,' it is definitely implied the man of sin would rise to power in the same place Caesar ruled: Rome!

"On the basis of these things, then, we know where the man of sin would rise to power and we know when! Where? He would rise to power in the place the Caesars ruled at the time Paul wrote his epistle; that is, Rome. The man of sin would be a Roman power! When would the man of sin be revealed? Upon the fall of the Roman Empire (under the rule of the Caesars) the man of sin would be revealed.

"Looking into history then, *who* followed the Caesars as rulers of Rome? What power rose up in Rome following the fall of the Empire? Many believed the evidence pointed to the Papacy. There was no other power that rose up at the time and place specified by the prophecy.

"**Barnes** has well said: 'To any acquainted with the decline and fall of the Roman Empire, nothing can be more manifest than the correspondence of the facts in history respecting the rise of the Papacy, and the statement of the apostle Paul here. (24)

'The mighty Caesars had fallen; Augustus, Domitian, Hadrian, Diocletian, were gone; even the Constantines and Julians had passed away. The seat of sovereignty had been removed from Rome to Constantinople. Goths and Vandals had overthrown the western empire; the once mighty political structure lay shivered into broken fragments. The imperial government was slain by the Gothic sword. The Caesars were no more, and Rome was an actual desolation. Then slowly on the ruins of old imperial Rome rose another power and another monarchy—a monarchy of loftier aspirations and more resistless might, claiming dominion, not alone over the bodies, but over the consciences and souls of men; dominion, not only within the limits of the fallen empire, but throughout the entire world. Higher and higher rose the Papacy, till in the dark ages all Christendom was subjected to its sway.' (27)

"The fact that the early Christians held the belief the 'let' or restraint was the Roman Empire, presents a problem for those who hold the futurist interpretation of prophecy. If that which was holding back the revelation of the man of sin was the Roman Empire, how could the man of sin be someone who would not appear until the very end of the age? Since the Roman Empire fell many centuries ago, what has been holding back his appearance all of these centuries since that time?

"To admit the 'let' was the Roman Empire is to admit that the prophecy of the man of sin has found fulfillment in the Pope, for it was the Papacy which rose up in the place and time designated by the prophecy. But futurism teaches the man of sin is some future individual—someone, in fact, who will not be revealed until after a supposed 'secret rapture!' Consequently, those who hold the dispensational viewpoint must ignore all of this evidence that the 'let' was the Roman Empire under the Caesars, and substitute a theory of modern origin.

"Those who hold the dispensational-futurist interpretation usually suggest a few vague possibilities and then end up saying the 'restraint' is the Holy Spirit in and through the Church. The following quotations from dispensational writers are typical of many; 'The hindering influence in this passage is, of course, the ministry of the Holy Spirit in and through the lives of Christians today.' (28) 'This One who hinders the man of sin must be the Holy Spirit. At the rapture of the saints, we believe, the Holy Spirit will be taken out of the way of the man of sin so that he may be revealed.' (29)

"This teaching is nothing but an echo from the theory spread by *Scofield* that the restrainer 'can be no other than the Holy Spirit in the Church, to be "taken out of the way".' (30) But as *Oswald Smith* has well said concerning the verse under consideration: 'There is no mention of the Holy Spirit at all. That is a *Scofield Bible* assumption. The Holy Spirit and the church remain to the end of the age.' (31)

"We all recognize, of course, that the Holy Spirit within the church is a great force against evil in the world, but this was not the 'let' of which Paul spoke. Paul told the Thessalonians the day of Christ's coming and our gathering together unto him could not take place until *after* the man of sin would be revealed (2 Thessalonians 2:1-3). Surely then, he would not turn right around in the same chapter and contradict himself by teaching that the church is the 'let' which must be taken out of the way before the man of sin would be revealed! This would be the exact opposite of what he had just said!

"The teaching that the church would be taken out of the world before the man of sin is revealed is absolutely contrary to what all Christian teachers and preachers have always taught—until this century! Though they may have differed on details, they all envisioned the Antichrist as a persecuting power against the true believers—a power that would make war against the saints! On this they were united. None of them thought of the church as being absent from the earth during the reign of Antichrist.

63

"We have seen that Paul was careful not to mention the restraint by name when writing to the Thessalonians. But if the restraint had been the Holy Spirit or the church, there would have been no reason for Paul not to mention this in 2 Thessalonians 2. Several times in his writings to the Christians at Thessalonica, he mentioned the church (1 Thessalonians 1:1; 2:14; 2 Thessalonians 1:1, 4) and he also mentioned the Holy Spirit (1 Thessalonians 1:5, 6; 4:8; 5:19; 2 Thessalonians 2:13).

"Those who believe that the Holy Spirit will be taken out of this world are faced with serious problems of interpretation. They teach after the church is gone, God will turn to the Jews, a believing remnant of which will preach the gospel of the kingdom into all the world. They will be so empowered, some ask us to believe, they 'will become the mightiest evangelists this world has ever seen.' (33)

"But who, we ask, will so empower these Jews if the Holy Spirit is taken from the earth? How could they evangelize the world if the Holy Spirit, which convicts and converts, is gone? Is there some other agent more powerful than the Spirit of God?

"We find no proof whatsoever in the scriptures for the belief that the 'let' was the Holy Spirit or the church. On the other hand, there are very good reasons for believing that the Roman Empire under the rule of the Caesars was that which was to be taken out of the way. That is, the Roman Empire would be broken up and fall—then the man of sin would be revealed in power."

1. Rice, Worldwide War and the Bible, p. 212.
6. Froom, The Prophetic Faith of Our Fathers, p. 19.
14. Chrysostom, Homilies, pp. 388, 389.
19. Vol. 2, p. 60 (1961 Ed.), Article: Antichrist.
20. Note on 2 Thessalonians 2.

21. *Tanner, Daniel and Revelation, pp. 188, 189.*
22. *Jerome, Commentaria, Bk. 5, chapter 25.*
23. *Chrysostom, Homilies, p. 388, 389.*
24. *Barnes' Commmentary, p. 1115.*
27. *Guinness, Romanism and the Reformation, p. 61.*
28. *Orr, Antichrist, Armageddon, and the End of the World, p. 11.*
29. *Rice, The Coming Kingdom of Christ, p. 125.*
30. *Scofield Reference Bible, p. 1272.*
31. *Smith, Tribulation or Rapture—Which? p. 8.*
33. *Appleman, Antichrist and the Jew, p. 12.*

The following is another understanding of 2 Thessalonians 2:1-7:

"With great desire we await the dawning of that new day, when His kingdom shall be established in the earth, and righteousness shall flourish in our land. Hence one watches for the fulfillments of the signs which point to the nearness of that time. Some signs are negative, some positive.

"*'Come a falling away...'* Literally, the apostasy, the total desertion of principles or faith. Compromise is the order of the day, lawlessness the spirit of the times. We need not expand on this, it is happening everywhere. Along with this *'falling away,'* the man of sin must be revealed. But herein lies the glorious truth, that wicked one cannot be fully revealed until something else has also happened. *'And now ye know what withholdeth that he might be revealed in his time.'* (verse 6). *Withholdeth*—literally, *hold down.* There is a restraining force that holds the powers of hell at bay, so that they cannot release their full scope of power and havoc, until... *'For the mystery of iniquity* (lawlessness) *doth already work: only he who now letteth will let, until he be taken out of the way.'* (verse 7).

"*Letteth*—again the Greek word to *'hold down,'* or

restrain, thus the Clementson trans. *'there is one who restraineth now, until he may* **become** *from the midst.* Where King James Version gives *'be taken out'* of the way, the Greek word is, **to become.** Here is the positive counterbalance to all the negativity of the mystery of iniquity. There is that which is **becoming from the midst**, it is now in the process of being formed and brought to maturity, and until it has fully become, all else is held in restraint.

"The *'tares and the wheat'* are both growing to maturity, both in the process of becoming, and though He will *'gather* **first** *the tares,'* yet the final climax cannot occur until the **sons of God have become from the midst.** *Present restraints are in order for their protection, until God had finished His work in them and then shall the end of this age be consummated."*

Ralph Woodrow also puts to rest the "two phase" return of Jesus:

"On the subject of Bible prophecy, most of the Christians I knew had been influenced by the 'dispensational' interpretation of prophecy as taught in the notes of the *Scofield Bible.* There was a lot of talk about the 'rapture.' Though the word did not actually appear in the Bible, I found it was commonly used to described that time when believers would be *'caught up...in the clouds, to meet the Lord in the air'* (1 Thessalonians 4:17). But the question was: Would this 'catching up' or 'rapture' be a separate event from the return of Christ at the end of the age?

"According to the dispensational outline, Christ would return in two separate events—first in the air, before the tribulation, to gather His own (the rapture)—and then, at the end of the tribulation period, He would come again, this time openly and in glory (the revelation). Thus, the rapture was set in contrast to the *revelation* and *two* second comings (or two stages of the second coming) were taught.

"I once read the entire New Testament through to see if I could find any scriptures that taught the return of Jesus would be in two stages. We have a tract available (upon request) which lists all the verses I found. When one opens the tract, 'All Scriptures that Teach the Return of Christ will be in Two Stages,' its pages are blank!

"In time I would learn that not only was the two-stage return of Christ not found in the Bible, according to history it was not taught during the early century of the church; it was not taught by any of the reformers such as Luther, Calvin, or Wesley; it was not taught by anyone until around a century and a half ago! It has been a puzzle to me how some will contend for the old time faith in other areas, yet hold a viewpoint that did not surface until comparatively modern times concerning the return of Christ!

"When I questioned some who believed in the two-stage teaching, the verses they quoted seemed very weak and unconvincing. I was told, for example, that Revelation 4:1 was a clear picture of the rapture when John saw a vision of a door opened in heaven and heard a voice say, 'Come up hither.' But John could not be a consistent type of the church being raptured to heaven, for he was (as it were) sometimes on earth, in the wilderness, on the sands of the sea, or back in heaven as the various scenes unfolded.

"Some told me that the rapture had to be a separate coming, for in the rapture Christ would come secretly, quietly— 'as a thief in the night.' But a study of all the 'thief' passages failed to indicate a separate coming. Instead, these passages showed that his coming would be like a thief only in the sense that the *time* was unrevealed. It would overtake the world unexpectedly, but even this did not apply to true believers: 'Ye, brethren, are not in darkness, that the day should overtake you as a thief,' (1 Thessalonians 5:4).

"I discovered that the two best-known 'thief' passages did

67

not indicate a quiet event at all. If anything, just the reverse was implied. In one, Paul spoke of the Lord coming with a **shout**, the **voice** of the archangel, and the **trump** of God as believers would be caught up to meet the Lord in the air (1 Thessalonians 4:16, 17). This did not sound like a quiet event to me. In the other passage, Peter spoke of Christians 'looking' for the Lord's coming, stating that the day of the Lord would come as a thief in the night and the heavens would *pass away with a great* **noise!**' (2 Peter 3:4-12).

"Another argument was that two second comings were taught 'in the Greek.' One writer whose books were being widely circulated at the time made this statement: 'The *two* phases of Christ's second coming are clearly distinguished in the Greek. The "parousia"...is his coming for his saints...The "apokalupsis" (the revealing, unveiling, making manifest) is his coming with his saints,'—seven years later. I was to later find, however, that no such distinction was taught in the Greek at all. The church I attended at age 15 had given me a Strong's Concordance (because I mowed the lawns around the church building each week). In this concordance I looked up—for myself—all of the various Greek words such as 'parousia' and 'apokalupsis.' I found that instead of these words making a distinction, they were actually used *interchangeably*.

"While it was true that Paul spoke of 'the coming (parousia) of the Lord,' in the noted rapture passage (1 Thessalonians 4:15-17), he also said that Christ would destroy the man of sin with 'the brightness of his coming (parousia),' (2 Thessalonians 2:1-17). This placed the parousia after the reign of the man of sin—not before.

"Peter spoke of 'the promise of His coming (parousia)' as being fulfilled in that day when 'the heavens shall pass away with a great noise, and the elements shall melt with fervent heat,' (2 Peter 3:4-12). None applied this passage

68

to a so-called pre-tribulation rapture—yet the word, 'parousia' was used here.

"I also looked up the references in which the other word, 'apokalupsis,' was used. But none of these indicated a later coming of Christ as distinct from his 'parousia.' In 2 Thessalonians 1:7-10, I read: *'The Lord Jesus shall be revealed* (apokalupsis) *from heaven with his mighty angels, in flaming fire taking vengenance on them that know not God...when he shall* **come** *to be glorified in his saints.'* If this rapture was an earlier event, seven years before, the saints would have already been glorified!

"Christians are pictured as *'waiting for the coming* (apokalupsis) *of our Lord Jesus,'* (1 Corinthians 1:7). If the 'apokalupsis' is a separate coming seven years after the 'parousia' as some suppose—how could Christians be waiting for the 'apokalupsis?' They could not be waiting on the 'apokalupsis,' if they had already been raptured seven years before at the 'parousia!'

"In Matthew 24:37, I read of the *'coming* (parousia) *of the Son of Man,'* while in Luke's account of the same passage I noticed he used apokalupsis, *'when the Son of man is revealed* (apokalupsis),' (Luke 17:26, 30). Seeing these things, it was clear to me that the idea of two separate second comings of Christ could not be based on the Greek. If anything, the way these words were used interchangeably, *one* event was indicated, not two!"

Another rapture contention is: ''If we are not going to be 'caught up' to heaven in a rapture, why does God's Word tell us so much about it in the many heavenly scenes as in the book of the Revelation?'' The answer to that question is in the prayer the Lord taught us to pray; ''When (not, if) your Kingdom has come (to the earth) and Your will (and purpose) has been done *on earth* as it now is in heaven...'' So, He is simply showing us what it is going to be like here on earth.

Remember, there shall be a *"new heaven and a new earth, wherein dwelleth righteousness,"* (when *all* the wicked and evil have been destroyed)," 2 Peter 3:13 and Revelation 21:1, 5. Also the *"New Jerusalem"* (God's divine order) is *"coming **down*** *(to earth)* (Revelation 3:12: 21:2). Those who insist on *going up* would miss this fulfillment (answer) to the constant prayer that Lord taught us to pray. We get more understanding on this earthly kingdom in Revelation 5:9, 10: *"And they sung a new song, saying, 'Thou art worthy to take the book, and to open the seals thereof: for thou wast slain, and hast redeemed us to God by thy blood out of every kindred, and tongue, and people, and nations; And hast made us unto our God kings and priests: and **we** shall reign on the earth.'"* And Revelation 11:15, *"...there were great voices in heaven, saying, 'The kingdoms of this world **are become** the kingdoms of our Lord, and of His Christ; and He shall reign forever and ever.'"* Also Revelation 20:4, *"...and they lived and reigned with Christ a thousand years."*

Scriptures make it so very obvious that God the Father is far more interested in getting heaven *into* you, than getting *you* into heaven.

Another most grievous deception of the rapture frame of mind is that the rapture is their blessed hope. The Scripture they quote is Titus 2:13, *"Looking for that **blessed hope** and the glorious **appearing** of our **great God and Savior Jesus Christ**."* Rapture is their false hope, not the second coming of Jesus Christ to live and reign the *"Kingdoms of this world" "forever and ever!"* (Rev. 11:15—The Hallelujah Chorus!)

This Scripture tells us clearly that we are to look for the *appearing* Christ, *not* the *disappearing* saints!

7

Origin of Rapture

With God's Word so very clear on the fact that there will *not* be a rapture, where did this doctrine, opposed to the doctrines of 19 *previous* centuries, originate?

Several individuals have researched an answer to this question and all arrive at the same conclusion as to its origin.

The most complete books on the subject, known to me are: *The Incredible Cover-Up,* by *Dave MacPherson of Omega Publications, P.O. Box 4130, Medford, Oregon, 97501* and a later one, *The Great Rapture Hoax* by *Dave MacPherson of New Puritan Library, 91 Lytle Road, Fletcher, North Carolina 28732.*

It *is a fact* that no Christian churches, congregations or fellowships existing prior to 1830 proclaimed a rapture doctrine, and all accepted the Biblical truth that Christians would be on earth during the time of great tribulation. Before 1830, the single rapture scriptures of 1 Thessalonians 4:13-18 were accepted as resurrection verses: *"Brothers, we do not want you to be ignorant about those who are asleep* (dead in Christ)'' (NIV, verse 13). They did *not* see these verses as an escape from the earth to heaven, as we have seen from the *whole council* of God's Word; clearly the correct understanding of these verses.

Some of the pre-1830 writers quoted by *Dave MacPherson* are: 1) *Augustine* (354-430), ''But he who reads this passage (Dan. 12), even half asleep, cannot fail to see that the kingdom of Antichrist shall fiercely, though for a short time, *assail the Church...*'' (*The City of God*, XX, 23).

2) *John Wycliffe* (1320-1384), ''Wherefore let us pray to God that He keep us in the hour of temptation, which is coming upon *all* the world,'' (*Writings of the Reverend and Learned John Wycliffe*, p. 155).

3) *John Calvin* (1509-1564), ''...We ought to follow in our inquires after Antichrist, especially where such *pride* proceeds to a *public desolation of the Church*,'' (*Institutes*, Vol. 2, p. 411).

4) *Martin Luther* (1483-1546), ''The book of Revelation is intended as a revelation of things that are to happen in the future and *especially of tribulations and disasters for the Church...*'' (*Works of Martin Luther*, VI, p. 481).

5) *George Mueller* (1805-1898), ''The Scripture declares plainly that the Lord Jesus will *not* come until the *Apostacy* shall have taken place...'' (*Mission Tours and Labors*, p. 148).

6) *Benjamin W. Newton* (1805-1898), ''The Secret Rapture was bad enough, but this (John Darby's equally novel idea that the book of Matthew is on 'Jewish' ground instead of 'Church' ground) was even worse,'' (*Prophetic Developments*, p. 29).

7) *Dale Moody*, ''There is not a passage in the New Testament to support Scofield. The call to John to 'come up hither' has reference to mystical ecstasy, *not* to a pretribulation rapture,'' (*Spirit of the Living God*, p. 203).

8) *C.S. Lovette*... "I no longer teach Christians they will *not* have to go through the tribulation," (*PC*, January, 1974).

9) *Billy Graham*, "Perhaps the Holy Spirit is getting His Church ready for *a trial and tribulation such as the world has never known*," (San Shoemaker's *Under New Management*, p. 72).

Knowing that the rapture doctrine only appeared after about 1830-1840, indicated a time for its origin.

Dave MacPherson, after a complete and scholarly research on the origin of the rapture doctrine is able to write, "After taking all available facts into consideration, I can say it occurred on an unknown evening between February 1st and April 14th in 1830." He traces this rapture doctrine's origin back to *Margaret Macdonald* of *Port Glasgow, Scotland*, (documentation in his "The Incredible Cover-Up").

Through visits to *Margaret Macdonald, John Darby,* organizer and promoter of the Plymouth Brethren movement, received this new revelation of a Pre-Tribulation Rapture.

He expanded and promoted it and a two-phased Second Coming of the Lord Jesus Christ, to include a secret rapture. He did not seem to consider the fact that a secret rapture was so secret the Church had not heard of it, not discovered it, in Scripture for over 1800 years!

Then, *Edward Irving* of the *Catholic Apostolic Church*, a contemporary of *Darby*, accepted the Pre-Trib Rapture doctrine in spite of the fact that he and all Christians before him had accepted and taught the "day of the Lord" would not begin until *after* the Tribulation.

Next, this doctrine was accepted by an American, *C.I. Scofield*, who included it in his very popular annotated/footnoted Bible. Another American, *Finus Dake*, also promoted the rapture doctrine in his annotated Bible and commentaries.

With these references, many so-called fundamentalist churches have included a rapture in their doctrines and taught it in their seminaries and Bible schools.

In preceding chapters, we have compared Scripture with Scripture to answer the question, "Will Biblical Christians be removed from the earth to heaven in a rapture?" The Scriptures are consistent in making it ever so clear that the answer is, *"No"*

Corrie ten Boom stated it correctly when she said, "The rapture doctrine is a false teaching that *Jesus warned us* to expect in the latter days," (***Logos Journal***, Nov.-Dec. 1974, p. 20).

The wide and rapid acceptance of such an obviously false doctrine of escapism through a rapture is foretold in 2 Timothy 4:3, 4, NIV, *"For the time will come when men will not put up with sound doctrine. Instead, to suite their own desires, they will gather around them a great number of teachers to say what their itching ears want to hear. They will turn their ears away from the truth and turn aside to myths."* The Word of God shows rapture to be one of those myths, because Jesus always told us *"plainly"* what He wanted us to know!

The rapture escape-type doctrine seems clearly the subject of Jeremiah 14:13, 14, NIV, *"But I said, 'Ah, Sovereign Lord,' the prophets keep telling them, 'You will not see the sword, or suffer famine. Indeed, I will give you lasting peace in this place.' Then the Lord said to me, 'The prophets are prophesying lies in My name. I have not sent them or appointed them or spoken to them. They are prophesying to you false visions, divination, futility and the delusions of their own minds."* The rapture doctrine sure seems to fit that description; as well as some other movements that had their beginning in the same century.

Indeed, it is interesting to note that, while the 19th century was a time of great revival in the church, we know from scriptures that for every move of the Holy Spirit, there is a counter move of Satan; thus, also in the 19th century, besides Margaret MacDonald, and the rapture movement, the 19th century also saw the Christian Science movement, Jehovah's Witnesses, and the Morman Church.

Each of these had "new, divine visions" and "further words from God" that no early disciple or apostle, or even Jesus Himself spoke of!

One of the warnings to the Church in Thyatira, was about a "false prophetess" (Rev. 2:20-22) and those who followed her: *"Notwithstanding I have a few things against thee, because thou sufferest that woman Jezebel which calleth herself a prophetess, to teach and seduce my servants, to commit fornication, and eat things sacrificed unto idols. And I gave her space to repent of her fornication; and she repented not. Behold, I will cast her into a bed, and them that com-mit* (spiritual) *adultary with her into great tribulation, except they repent of their deeds."*

How do we know *who* has committed spiritual adultary? We are warned at the end of the Bible, Rev. 22:18, 19: *"For I testify unto every man that heareth the words of the prophecy of this book, 'If any man shall add* (rap-ture?) *unto these things, God shall add unto him the plagues that are written in this book; and if any man shall take away from the words* (our time of patient suf-fering and cleansing *through* tribulation as victorious over-comers?) *of the book of prophecy, God shall take away his part out of the book of life and out of the holy city, and from the things which are written in this book.'"*

Surely a merciful God, who doesn't want *any* to perish would have *plainly* told us such an important thing as to whether or not we should *be prepared* to suffer and be pa-tient *through* the tribulation. Jesus did in Matt. 24:4-13, NIV, *"Jesus said: 'Watch out that no one deceives you...then you will be handed over to be persecuted*

75

and put to death...At that time, many will turn away from the faith (the great falling away) *and betray and hate each other, and many false prophets will appear and deceive many people. Because of the increase of wickedness, the love of many will grow cold, but he who stands firm to the end will be saved.'''*

Certainly we must be very careful whom we believe. This is every Christian's responsibility to search the scriptures himself to *"see if these things be true."*

Knowing that God does *not* change in His dealing with mankind, we would do well to heed Romans 1:25 and 28 (NIV). *"They exchanged the truth of God for a lie...since they did not think it worthwhile to retain the knowledge of God, He gave them over to a depraved* (reprobate) *mind, to do what ought not be done."* Accepting false doctrine and perpetuating it can have very serious consequences!

As we have seen in previous chapters, those who accept the rapture doctrine have to reject at least fifty Scriptures that clearly state (requiring no interpretation, no inductive reasonings and no deductive reasonings) there will *not* be a removal of Biblical Christians from the earth to heaven in a rapture. God says in 2 Thessalonians 2:10-12 (NIV), *"They perish because they refused to love the truth and so be saved. For this reason God sends them a powerful delusion so that they will believe the lie and so that all will be condemned who have not believed the truth, but have delighted in their wickedness (deception)."*

They not only have to ignore all the no-rapture Scriptures, they have to support the rapture doctrine by taking Scriptures out of context, as in the case of *"the one is taken the other left,"* and distort other Scriptures, as in the case where the word, "church," does not appear after Revelation chapter 4, therefore, the church must have been removed in a rapture. God has something to say about such activities. 2 Peter 3:16 (NIV), *"His* (Paul's) *letters contain some things that are hard to understand, which ignorant and unstable people distort, as they do the other Scriptures, to their own destruction."* This could sure apply to Paul's writings in 1 Thessalonians 4:13-18!

Jesus rebuked the Pharisees and teachers saying, in Matthew 15:6 (NIV), *"...you nullify the Word of God for the sake of your traditions,* (doctrines).*"* And in Mark 7:8, 9 (NIV), *"You have let go of the commands of God and are holding on to the traditions* (doctrines) *of men. And He* (Jesus) *said to them, 'You have a fine way of setting aside the commands of God in order to observe your own traditions,'* (doctrines).*"*

We are admonished in Colossians 2:8 (NIV), *"See to it that no one takes you captive through hollow and deceptive philosophy, which depends on human traditions,* (doctrines).*"*

As we have mentioned in a previous chapter, many well-known evangelists and teachers of radio and television had broadcast and written books that the rapture would occur 14 May 1981. When that did not come to pass, the date for the great Christian lift-off was changed to 28 June 1981, but, no go! They issued a forty day correction (Noah's forty days of rain), to delay the heavenly launch, countdown to 7 August 1981. Still no launch. And even today, seven years later, people still listen to and finance these same teachers of rapture!

Another wrote a letter to his mailing list of at least one million telling them they need not worry nor fear a nuclear/atomic war (as depicted in the TV propaganda horror show, "The Day After") because they would all be raptured up to heaven before it happened.

And even those who added forty years (a generation) to

the latter days birthdate of Israel on 14 May 1948, to set 14 May 1988 as their estimated time of departure were, by the Word of the Lord, still here on 15 May 1988! The latest book *88 Reasons The Rapture Will Be In 1988* set the first of his raptures for September 12, 1988. This same man has re-set his rapture date for September 1989. Can you think of one prophet or apostle, or even Jesus Himself, who gave a prophesy, then had to say, "Whoops, I made a mistake. What I really meant was..."? He is another end of this age false prophet Jesus mentions in Matthew 24:11, *"And many false prophets shall arise, and shall deceive many."* (Remember, John told us if someone prophesies something, *test the spirits* [wait and see if it comes to pass] to know if that one is truely a prophet. I John 4:1, 2 Pe. 2:1.)

And even if we calculate it was two thousand years from Adam to Abraham and two thousand years from Abraham to Jesus and two thousand years from Jesus to the millennium of Revelation 20, it makes for a total of six thousand years from Adam to the millennium. If we make these six thousand years to be six days as per 2 Peter 3:8 and Psalm 90:4 *"With the Lord a day is as a thousand years"*, the seventh day is the millennium, which would start approximately in the year 2000, according to this method of counting.

By the Word of God, we can be very sure that those Biblical Christians who are alive at that time will still be right here on the earth/world. By the year 2001, I trust the rapture doctrine will have departed from God's creation.

As we know, Jesus warned us that we could expect *"...false Christs and false prophets...if it were possible they shall deceive the very elect,"* (Matthew 24:24). We saw in Romans 1, 2 Thessalonians 2, and 2 Peter 3, some distort and reject the truth and believe a lie, clinging to doctrines of men, (Mark 7:8). However, there is good news in Daniel 12:4 (Amplified Bible), *"But you, O*

Daniel, shut up the words and seal the book until the time of the end. (Then) *many shall run to and fro and search anxiously* (through the Book)*, and knowledge* (of God's purposes as revealed by His prophets) *shall be increased and become great.''* I trust *those* days are *these* days!

8

What May Happen

The answer to the question, "What will happen?" can only be found in the Holy Scriptures. Let us explore some possible answers to that question.

As has been stated before, the ultimate objective is the answer to the prayer the Lord Jesus taught us to pray: *"Our Father in heaven, hallowed be Your name, (when) Your kingdom* (has) *come, Your will (will have been) be done, on earth as it is* (now) *in heaven,"* (Matthew 6:9, 10 NIV).

We see the fulfillment and answer to this prayer in Revelation 21:2, 3, *"And I, John, saw the holy city, new Jerusalem, coming* **down** *from God out of heaven, prepared as a bride adorned for her husband. And I heard a great voice out of heaven saying, 'Behold the tabernacle of* **God is with men** *and He will* **dwell with them,** *and they shall be His people, and God Himself shall* **be with them,** *and be their God.'"* "God Himself" comes to us, we do not go to Him! This is also an answer and fulfillment of the prayer of Jesus in John 17:21, *"That they* (all believers) *may be one; as Thou, Father, art in me, and I in Thee, that they may also be one in Us..."*

The "New Jerusalem" is clearly symbolic of God's divine will or order coming to the earth. In Bible numerics, the number twelve is associated with God's divine order, will, and/or government.

In Revelation 21:12-17 we learn that the new/holy city Jerusalem: *"...had a wall great and high, and had twelve gates, and at the gates twelve angels, and names written thereon, which are the names of the twelve tribes of the children of Israel...And the wall of the city had twelve foundations, and in them the names of the twelve apostles of the Lamb...And he measured the city with the reed, twelve thousand furlongs. The length and the breadth, and the height of it are equal. And he measured the wall thereof, an hundred and forty and four cubits..."* (144 = 12 x 12) As we can see, the New Jerusalem is multiples of God's divine will, government and order coming to earth. Then all the *"former things are passed away...all things are new,"* (Rev. 21:4, 5).

Remember, the New Jerusalem is coming down to earth (Rev. 3:12) ...going up in a rapture would cause us to miss this greatest of blessings and the answer to the prayer the Lord taught us to pray!

"And they shall not teach every man his neighbour, and every man his brother, saying, 'Know the Lord': for all shall know Me, from the least to the greatest," (Hebrews 8:11).

Also, (For it is written) (Isa. 45:23) *"I have sworn by myself...every knee shall bow, every tongue shall swear,"* (confess to God).

If "all shall know the Lord" and "every knee shall bow

81

to the Lord and every tongue shall confess to God," what became of the wicked/unrighteous? They have either been converted to a faith in Jesus Christ the Lord, or destroyed during the tribulation as foretold by Jesus in His many examples of "the wicked shall be taken, destroyed, severed, or converted from among the just or righteous." And when all the wicked have been converted or destroyed, we shall have a "new heaven and a new earth" and "all things are new." This is the earth the righteous inherit, and the *"heaven on earth"* of Revelation!

But what about us as individuals? The Scriptures tell us. We are to become like Jesus! *"...We know that when He* (Jesus) *shall appear, we shall be like Him, for we shall see Him as He is,"* (1 John 3:2). And in 1 John 4:17, NIV, *"Because in this world we are like Him,* (Jesus)*."* *"When the Chief Shepherd appears, you will receive the crown of glory that will never fade away,"* (1 Pet. 5:4, NIV). Also in Colossians 3:4, NIV, *"When Christ, who is your life, appears, then you also will appear with Him in glory." "When He* (Jesus) *shall come to be glorified in His saints,"* (2 Thess. 1:10).

How will this come to pass? The Scriptures tell us. 1 Thessalonians 5:23, 24, NIV, (May) *"...the God of peace sanctify you through and through. May your whole spirit, soul and body be kept blameless at the coming of our Lord Jesus Christ* (not at our 'going' to Christ!)*. The one who calls you is faithful, and he will do it."* And in Philippians 1:6, NIV, *"Being confident of this, that He who began a good work in you will carry it on to completion until the day of Jesus Christ."* (Here again, *not* the day we are raptured!) And in Ephesians 4:12-13, NIV, *"...so that the body of Christ may be built up until we all reach unity in the faith and in the knowledge of the Son of God and become* (complete) *mature, attaining the whole measure of the* *fullness of Christ.''*

We need tribulation to bring us unto completion/maturity, according to the Scriptures. Jesus assures us in John 16:33, *"In the world **you shall have tribulation: but be of good cheer; I have overcome the world.''** Remember, "Greater is He that is **in you,** than he that is in the world,''* (1 John 4:4). We find in Acts 14:22, *"...Exorting them to continue in the faith and that **we must through much tribulation** enter into the kingdom of God.''*

For those who have believed that they were going to escape the great tribulation in a fly-away rapture, it would be well to *review* the tribulation Scriptures they have ignored in the past.

What is tribulation? As you may know, the King James Version (KJV) of New Testament was translated from a Latin version, which was translated from the Greek language. You can find in *Young's* or *Strong's Concordance*, the Greek word, *thilipsis* appears fifty-five times in the KJV and is translated into *nine* different English words: Tribulation—21, affliction—17, dead—9, trouble—3, anguish—1, persecution—1, burdened—1, die—1, and to be afflicted—1. Very confusing! A translation of the word, *thilipsis* consistent with its use and meaning in the Bible would be, "a time of testing.'' This gives a much clearer understanding of what God is saying to us.

As the rapture proponents have made much of their escaping the *great thilipsis,* let us review those Scriptures:

In Matthew 24:21 Jesus says, *"**For then** (at the end of the age) **there shall be great** (extreme/severe) **tribulation** (time of testing), **such as was not since the beginning of the world to this time, no, nor ever shall be.''** The next verse tells us that Christians are *in* the great time of testing. *"**And except those days be shortened, there should no flesh be saved: but for the elect's sake** (there is no way you can make this say, Jews!—we are clearly told over and over *we* are the elect), **these days will be shortened.**" We should note that the words, "great tribulation," only appear here, and in Revelation 2:22, which is *not* in the same context. (And God *is* speaking to the *church* in Rev. 2:22, talking about a female prophetess who taught spiritual adultary to some of the *church*.) Yet, the "pre-trib" teachers make much of this single verse, as their whole rapture doctrine is based on the single verse of 1 Thessalonians 4:17.

To gain an understanding of the purpose of times of testing, (tribulation) we shall look at some other Scriptures.

We are referred to the prophet Daniel by our Lord Jesus Christ, in Matthew 24:15, for additional understanding of events/signs of "the end of the age" and "the coming of the Son of Man." Daniel often uses the term, "the time of the end." In the Amplified Bible we read in Daniel 11:35, **"...and then the insincere among the people will lose courage and become deserters** (the "falling away" of 2 Thess. 2:3). **It shall be a test to refine, to purify and make those among God's people pure, even to the time of the end.**" And in 1 Peter 1:7 we are told, **"The trying** (testing) **of your faith is much more precious than gold—that you may be pure at the coming of Jesus Christ.**" Yes, we can expect times of testing (tribulation) in these latter days; they are for our growth unto mature Christians. Consider Romans 5:3-5, AMP, **"...we glory in** (times of testing) **tribulations also, knowing that** (testing) **tribulations worketh patience; and patience, experience; and experience, hope. And hope maketh not ashamed; because the love of God is shed abroad in our hearts by the Holy Ghost** (Spirit) **which is given to us.**" And in James 1:2-4 we are told, **"count it all joy when ye fall into divers** (diverse) **temptations** (testings)**; knowing this, that the trying of your faith worketh patience. But let** *patience have her perfect/complete work, that you may be perfect* (complete)*, and entire, wanting nothing."*

Now that we see that "times of testing" (tribulation) of our faith produces patience, let us review the eight steps/phases to becoming a mature/complete Biblical Christian in 2 Peter 1:5-7, *"...giving all diligence, add to your faith,[1] virtue; and to virtue,[2] knowledge; and to knowledge,[3] temperance* (no excesses)*; and to temperance,[4] patience; and to patience,[5] godliness; and to godliness,[6] brotherly kindness,[7] and to brotherly kindness,[8]* (God-like love) *charity,[9]* (charity/Agape)*."*

"For if you possess these qualities in increasing measure, they will keep you from being ineffective and unproductive in your knowledge of our Lord Jesus Christ. But if anyone does not have them, he is nearsighted and blind, and has forgotten that he has been cleansed from his past sins," NIV, 2 Peter 1:8, 9.

In Hebrews 5:8, 9, *"Though He* (Jesus) *were a Son, yet learned He obedience by the things which He suffered/endured/experienced. And being made perfect/complete, He became the author of eternal salvation unto all them that obey Him."* Jesus is our example! And Jesus has told us that we "shall have times of testing (tribulation), but to be of good cheer because He has overcome." We are also to be overcomers! *"And he that overcometh and keepeth My works unto the end, to him I will give power over the nations,"* Jesus promises us in Revelation 2:26.

We are promised in 1 Corinthians 10:13 in the Amplified Bible, *"God is faithful to His word and to His compassionate nature not to let you be tested/tempted* (tribulated) *beyond your ability, strength of resistance and power to endure* (overcome)*."* As I mentioned earlier in the book, prisoners of war (POW) held by Godless communists during and after the wars in Korea and Vietnam, who had or gained a saving knowledge of our Lord Jesus Christ endured and survived (overcame), while some of those of no faith often compromised with the enemy or perished. History is filled with similar examples.

The 23rd Psalm is not a Psalm for the dead or dying. It is a promise to the living! *"Yea, though I walk through the valley of the shadow of death, I will fear no evil for Thou art with me...Surely goodness and mercy shall follow me all the days of my life."*

There is more good news for Biblical Christians. *"And there shall be a time of trouble* (tribulation)*, such as never was since there was a nation even to that same time* (the time of the end)*: and at that time thy people shall be delivered* (protected in it)*, everyone that shall be found written in the book. And many of them that sleep in the dust of the earth* (the dead) *shall awake* (be resurrected)*, some to everlasting life and some to everlasting shame and everlasting contempt."* This sounds like New Testament, but is Daniel 12:1, 2! Note that "the time of trouble" *and* the deliverance of God's people *and* the ressurection of the dead are all happening at the *same time*!

Psalm 37:32-40, *"The wicked watcheth the righteous, and seeketh to slay him. The Lord will not leave him in his hand, nor condemn him when he is judged. Wait on the Lord, and keep His way, and He shall exalt thee to inherit the land; when the wicked are cut off* (destroyed), (the tares)*, thou shalt see it* (no rapture)*. I have seen the wicked in great power, and spreading himself like a green bay tree. Yet, he passed away* (was destroyed)*, and, lo, he was not; yea, I sought him* (the wicked) *but he could not be found. Mark the perfect* (complete) *man, and behold the* *upright; for the end of that man is peace. But the transgressors shall be destroyed together; the end of the wicked shall be cut off* (tares) (destruction). *But the salvation of the righteous is of the Lord; He is their strength in the time of trouble* (tribulation). *And the Lord shall help them, and deliver them; He shall deliver them from the wicked* (the Evil One)*, and shall save them, because they trust in the Lord."* Remember the prayer of our Lord Jesus Christ in John 17:15, NIV, *"My prayer is not that you take them* (the believers, v. 20) *out of the world, but that you protect them from the evil one."* That is most reassuring, because the prayers or our Lord Jesus Christ *will be answered!*

"Rapture" is *not* a Bible word, but *resurrection, transformation, transfiguration, changed, redemption* and *glorified*, are Bible words. Those who espouse the doctrine of rapture often equate these words to, rapture. This is a distortion of God's word. That should be so very clear now that we know scripture after scripture promising to help us *overcome tribulation!*

In the K.J.V. of the Bible, the Greek word, *metamorphoo* is translated: be changed, be transfigured, and be transformed. Again, confusion.

Remembering the Lord Jesus Christ is our example to emulate and follow, we should look at key events of His life as man on earth before His crucifixion, as an example for those who will be *"alive and remain."*

We learn of His being *metamorphoo*ed on the so-called Mountain of Transfiguration in the following Scriptures; Matthew 17:1, 2 and Mark 9:2, *"...And* (Jesus) *bringeth them up into an high mountain apart, and was transfigured before them..."* Luke 9:28b, 29, Jesus took them *"and went up into a mountain to pray. And as He prayed, the fashion of His countenance was altered* (transfigured).''

With these Scriptures on the transfiguration of our Lord Jesus Christ *before* His crucifixion, we can search the Scriptures to learn what will happen to us who may be *"alive and remain"* on earth at His coming, as He is clearly our example.

1 Corinthians 15:51-54, *"Behold, I shew you a mystery/secret; we shall not all* (die) *sleep, but we shall all be* (transfigured) *changed in a moment, in the twinkling of an eye at the last trump. For the trumpet shall sound, the dead shall be raised incorruptible, and we shall be* (transfigured) *changed. For this corruptible must* (clothe itself) *put on incorruption, and this mortal must put on immortality. So when this corruptible shall have put on incorruption, and this mortal shall have put on immortality, then shall be brought to pass the saying that is written,* (in Isa. 25:8), *Death is swallowed up in victory."* And, *"The last enemy that shall be destroyed is death,"* (1 Corinthians 15:26).

We know that an average, normal blinking/twinkling of an eye is about one tenth (1/10) of a second. That is how quickly we shall be changed/transformed/transfigured! However, the word, moment, may not be referring to a measure of time. In the Greek it is, *en atomo/atomos.* Could God be telling us that in a tenth of a second our atoms (atomical structure) will be *changed*? Apparently, the atomical structure of our Lord Jesus Christ had been changed to make it possible for Him to go through walls. *"...with doors locked for fear of the Jews, Jesus came and stood among them* (the disciples)*..."* (John 20:19, NIV). Remember, we are told that *"...we know that when He* (Jesus) *appears, we shall be like Him"* (1 John 3:2, NIV). Moses and Elijah also appeared with Jesus on the mountain of transfiguration (Matt. 17:3, Mark 9:4 and Luke

9:30). And many dead saints arose and appeared to many in the holy city after Jesus' resurrection, (Matt.27:52, 53).

A few years ago, we could not have understood this changing of our atomical structure. But, now, in the last days, man has begun to gain knowledge and an understanding of antimatter.

There have been many papers written on antimatter in recent years. The easiest understood for those not having a science background appeared in the July 1988 *Popular Science* magazine. This article states, "In 1928, only a handful of players made up the particle (atomic structure) world: the photon, electron and proton. It would somehow not have been proper to disturb this cozy array." After a review of historical research since 1928 in this field of science, it states that the previously known atomic structure particles have a "mirror image" in the antimatter realm and are "positron" for "positive electrons" and "antiproton." It has been established that the "antiproton has the same mass and spin, but the opposite charge and magnetic moment of the proton." The article concludes that "much of what is now held sacred in physics will have to be scrapped." Because, "In the atomic world, energies (atomic particle movement) do not exist over a continuous range, but at definite (and various) levels, like the rungs on a ladder." And "that a *whole new world of antimatter* is yet to be explored."

(With no rapture, many sacred false doctrines will also have to be scrapped and open a whole new world for some of Scriptural truth and understanding to be explored. For those who are *willing* to "search the scriptures" to see if "these things be true," it can only lead to growth and maturity as a Christian.)

The prophet Daniel tells us that during **"the time of the end many shall run to and fro** (multitudes of travelers) **and knowledge shall increase** (multiply/abound),**"** (Dan. 12:4).

89

No one can doubt that travel (running to and fro) has multiplied when the first commercial passenger jet aircraft, the British comet, first flew only a generation ago (1948 + 40 years) and in 1988, over 400 million airline tickets were sold in the United States alone. Some were flying from the United States to Europe faster than the speed of sound in the British-French Concord aircraft.

Scientific knowledge is doubling about every ten years.

Biblical revelations (knowledge/understand) will also multiply/abound, if we can destroy false doctrines.

By now it should be obvious that 1 Corinthians 15:51-54 and 1 Thessalonians 4:13-18 are both talking about the resurrection of the dead in Christ and the *transformation* of the living Biblical Christians! Amen!

Jesus Christ our Lord and our example was changed/transformed/transfigured right here *on earth*, "in the air" (*aer*: Extending no more than ten or fifteen feet above the surface of the earth—see Chapter 5 of this book). Therefore, the Biblical Christians who are *"alive and remain"* to the coming of our Lord Jesus Christ will also be changed/transformed/transfigured right here **on earth, "in the air."** At that same time the *"dead in Christ"* shall be resurrected and *"together...we shall forever and ever be with the Lord"* right here **on earth, "in the air."**

Recognizing there can only be *one* "forever and ever," then the resurrection and changing would be the beginning of the reign/rule of the Lord Jesus Christ and His saints *here on earth*, and the destruction of Satan/Devil. Revelation 11:15, **"And the seventh angel sounded** (his trumpet)**; and there were great voices in heaven ('The Lord Himself shall descend from heaven with a shout, with the voice of the archangel, and with the trump**(et) **of God,'** 1 Thess. 4:16) **saying, 'The kingdoms of this world have become the kingdom of our Lord** (Jesus Christ) **and of His Christ; and He**

90

(or They) **shall reign forever and ever'** (Greek: To the ages of the ages).''

We know that Jesus Christ is **Lord**. Could the phrase, "His Christ" include the resurrected and transformed Biblical Christians? I believe so, because we find in Revelation 2:26, **"He** (they) **that overcame** (remember you are to be an overcomer, not copping out in a rapture!), **and keep My works unto the end, to him** (them) **will I give power over nations** (kingdoms). **And he** (they) **shall rule with a rod of iron** (firm authority).'' Revelation 21:7, **"He** (they) **that overcomes shall inherit all things...''** Revelation 22:5b, **"...and they** (the servants of *God and of the Lamb*. v. 3) **shall reign forever and ever.''**

How do we become overcomers? Again the answer is in the Word of God. Some examples:

Ephesians 6:13, **"Wherefore take unto you the whole armour of God** (verses 14-17), **that you may be able to withstand in the evil day** (tribulation?), **and having done** (overcome) **all, to stand.''** Yes, *stand*, not rapture out! 1 Corinthians 14:8, **"For if the trumpet give an uncertain** (could this *uncertain* sound refer to those *unsure* if they are to stay and fight, or flee?!) **sound, who shall prepare himself for battle?''** Yes, *battle*, not, rapture! Revelation 12:11, **"And they** (the saints) **overcame him** (the Devil/Satan, v. 9) **by the blood of the Lamb, and the word of their testimony; and they love not their lives unto the death.''** Yes, they stood *in battle*, as over-comers! They were not afraid to die for Christ. Revelation 20:10 tells us what happens to the Devil/Satan, he **"was cast into the lake of fire and brimstone.''** Just as Revelation tells us of the rewards of the "overcomers" in the following Scriptures: Rev. 2:7, **"To him that over-cometh will I give to eat of the tree of life** (Gen. 2:9), **which is in the midst of the paradise of God.''** Rev. 2:11, **"He that overcometh shall not be hurt of the second**

91

*death." Rev. 2:17, "To him that **overcometh** will I give to eat hidden manna, and will give him a white stone, and in the stone a new name written, which no man knoweth except he that receiveth it." Rev. 2:26, 27, "And he that **overcometh** and keepeth My works unto the end, to him will I give power over the nations. And he shall rule them with a rod of iron." Rev. 3:5, "He that **overcometh**, the same shall be clothed in white raiment; and I will not blot out his name out of the book of life, but I will confess his name before My Father, and before His angels." Rev. 3:12, "Him that **overcometh** will I make a pillar in the temple of My God, and he shall go no more out. And I will write upon him the name of My God, and the name of the city of My God, which is New Jerusalem, which cometh down out of heaven from My God. And I will write upon him My new name." Rev. 3:21, "To him that **overcometh** will I grant to sit with Me in My throne, even as I also overcame and am set down with My Father in His throne." Rev. 21:7, "He that **overcometh** shall inherit all things and he shall be My son,* (manifested sons of God of Romans 8:19 and 29)." With such scriptures, can there be *any* doubt that we are to *overcome*? Webster's definition of *overcome*: 1. to get *the better of* in competition, 2. to *master, surmount, overwhelm*: 1. *to pour down on and bury beneath*, 2. *to crush, overpower*; can anyone seriously think that "rapture/flyaway" fits into *any* definition of overcome?!

In previous chapters we have cited Scriptures which assure us that our Father God will see us through all that can come upon the earth...remember Shadrach, Meshach and Abednego. There are also other Scriptures for us to remember.

In Ezekiel 9:4-6 we read, **"And the Lord said unto him** (his servant)**, 'Go through the midst of the city, through the midst of Jerusalem, and set a mark upon**

92

the foreheads of the men that sigh and that cry for all the abominations that be done in the midst thereof.' And to the others He said in mine hearing, 'Go ye after him through the city, and smite; let not your eye spare, neither have ye pity. Slay utterly old and young, both maids, and little children, and women: but do not come near any man upon whom is the mark; and begin at My sanctuary (sounds like judgement is going to begin at the church).*'''* Revelation 7:2, 3, *''And I saw another angel ascending from the east having the seal* (mark) *of the living God. And he cried with a loud voice to the four angels, to whom it was given to hurt the earth and the sea, saying, 'Hurt not the earth, neither the sea, nor the trees, until we have sealed* (marked) *the servants of our God in their foreheads.'''* Revelation 9:4, *''And it was commanded them that they should not hurt the grass of the earth, neither any green thing, neither any tree, but only those men which do not have the seal* (mark) *of God in their foreheads.''*

What is this mark/seal of God? It is the Holy Spirit! 2 Corinthians 1:20-22, *''For all the promises of God in Him* (Jesus Christ) *are yea, and in Him, Amen, unto the glory of God by us. Now He which establisheth us with you in Christ, and **hath anointed us**, is God. Who has also **sealed**/marked us and given the earnest of the* (Holy) *Spirit in our hearts.''* Ephesians 1:13, *''In* (Christ) *whom ye also trusted after that ye heard the word of truth, the gospel of your salvation. In whom also after ye believed, ye were **sealed**/marked with that Holy Spirit of promise, which is the earnest* (initial payment) *of our inheritance until the redemption of the **purchased possession**, unto the praise of His glory.''*

John 6:27, *''Labour not for the meat which perisheth, but for the meat which endureth unto everlasting life,* *which the Son of Man shall give unto you, for Him hath God the Father **sealed**/marked."* Ephesians 4:30, *"And grieve not the Holy Spirit of God, whereby ye are **sealed**/marked unto the **day of redemption**."*

What is the significance of the phrase, *"day of redemption"* to the Biblical Christian? It is not, "day of rapture!" redemption refers to the final phase of the full and complete salvation available to us through our Lord and Saviour Jesus Christ, and relates to our physical body. Remember, to *redeem* means to purchase with *a price*! No free rides!

To understand Scriptures, it is essential and basic for you to accept the fact that you are a three-part creation of God the Father. Genesis 1:26, *"**And God said, 'Let us make man in our image after our likeness'...**"* The "image" of God could be referring to His being one God composed of Father, Son and Holy Spirit. (Like a three-roomed house without walls.) You are also a three-part creation of God: Spirit (Greek: *pneuma*), soul (Greek: *psyche*), and body (Greek: *soma*). Your spirit is eternal. Your soul is your mind, will, intellect and emotions. Your spirit and soul reside in your body. Many preacher/teachers use spirit and soul as being the same. They are not synonymous terms! You are *a spirit*. You have *a soul*. You reside in *a body*.

Genesis 2:7, *"**The Lord God formed** (molded) **man of the dust of the ground, and breathed...the breath of life** (spirit) (into him) **and man became a living soul**."* 1 Corinthians 15:45, *"**It is written, 'The first man Adam was made a living soul; the last Adam was made a quickening spirit.'**"* 1 Thessalonians 5:23, 24, *"**And the very God of peace sanctify you wholly** (completely)**; and I pray your whole spirit and soul and body be preserved blameless unto the coming of our Lord Jesus Christ. He** (Jesus Christ) **is faithful to do it**."* Philippians 1:6, *"**Being confident of this very thing, that he which hath begun a good work in you will**"*

94

perform (complete) *it until the day of Jesus Christ.''*

Without this Biblical understanding of a three-phased, complete salvation, we could not grasp the meaning of Scriptures like 2 Corinthians 1:10, *"Who God hath* (has) *delivered us* (spirit), *...doth* (He is) *deliver*(ing) *us* (soul) *and He will yet deliver us* (body).*"* Please notice it is past tense for spirit salvation, present/on-going tense for soul salvation and future tense for body salvation. In 1 Peter 1:3-5, *"...by the resurrection of Jesus Christ from the dead, to an inheritance incorruptible, and undefiled, and that fadeth not away, reserved in heaven for you, who are kept by the power of God through faith unto salvation ready to be revealed* (fulfilled/completed/accomplished) *in the last time.''* A three-part salvation!

As stated above, the word, ''redemption'' refers/relates to body salvation, for a *complete* salvation for our spirit, our soul and our body. Romans 8:23 and 29, *"...we groan within ourselves, waiting for ...the redemption of our body...to be conformed* (changed) *to the image of His Son, that He* (Jesus) *might be the first born among many brethren.''* Philippians 3:20, 21, *"...the Savior, the Lord Jesus Christ who shall change our vile body* (to be) *like unto His glorious body...''* 1 John 3:2, *"We know that when He* (Jesus) *shall appear, we shall be like Him.''* 2 Thessalonians 1:10, *"Jesus shall come to be glorified in His saints,''* here on earth. In Luke 21:28 Jesus tells us that, *"And when these things* (signs of the end of times) *begin to come to pass, then look up* (do not be depressed) *your redemption draweth nigh.''* Yes, *redemption, not* rapture!

9

What We Must Do

When Saul of Tarsus, who became Saint Paul, had his encounter with our Lord on the road to Damascus, he asked two questions, *"Who art thou, Lord...What wilt Thou have me to do?"* (Acts 9:4-6) I trust you know the Lord Jesus Christ as your Savior and are allowing Him to rule and reign in your life as Lord. Now the question, "What must we do as Biblical Christians?" Now that we know, by the Holy Scriptures, we are *not* going to "fly away" to heaven in a rapture, the answer to this question becomes most important.

In Luke 19:13, Jesus tells us as His bond servants, to *"Occupy till I come"* (KJV). That sure does *not* sound like rapture! However, of all the versions of the Bible listed on the title page of this book, only the King James Version uses the word, *"occupy."* The other translations make it much clearer as to what we are to be doing and agree with the Amplified Bible, *"Calling ten of His* (own) *bond*

servants, He gave them ten minas (each equal to about one hundred days' wages), **and said to them, 'Buy and sell with these while I go and return.'"** The New International Version says it this way, **"He called ten of His servants and gave them ten minas. 'Put this money to work,' He said, 'until I come back.'"** However, Christians "buy and sell" with a different attitude than the heathen as expressed in 1 Corinthians 7:30, ...(they) **"buy something, as if it were not theirs to keep;** (they) **use things of the world, as if not engrossed in them. For this world in its present form is passing away"** (NIV). Christians are to possess things...things are *not* to possess them.

Remember, Saint Paul made and sold tents (Acts 18:3). Not a very spiritual activity, but he was being obedient to the words of Jesus. It has been well said, "Christians should be spiritually natural and naturally spiritual." Two excellent books on that subject are *"The Normal Christian Life"* and *"The Spiritual Man"* by *Watchman Nee*. We are to *be* witnesses for the Lord, Jesus Christ.

First, we must learn, and it is a learning process, to be totally led by the Holy Spirit, because **"As many as are led by the Spirit of God, they are the sons of God,"** (Romans 8:14). We are **"to be conformed to the image of His Son, that He** (Jesus Christ) **might be the firstborn among many brethren,"** (Romans 8:29).

Is it possible for us to become like Jesus? As impossible as it may seem to us in our present state, the Scriptures assure us that **"with God all things are possible,"** (Matthew 19:26). If you are interested in more understanding on this part of God's plan for man, there are two excellent books: *Become Like Jesus* by *Dr. James McKeever, Omega Ministries, P.O. Box 1788, Medford, OR 97501;* and *Jesus, The Pattern Son,* by *Bill Britton, P.O. Box 707, Springfield, MO 65801.*

In any and all our explorations into God's Word (the Scriptures) we must see to it the Lord Jesus Christ is central, preeminent, transcendent, supreme, and above *all.*

A clear and concise summation of the "good news" of the Gospel (God's Only Son Provides Eternal Life) is recorded in Philippians 2:5 through 11 (Amplified Bible), *"Let this same attitude and purpose and* (humble) *mind be in you which was in Christ Jesus—Let Him be your example in humility—Who, although being essentially one with God and the form of God* (possessing the fullness of the attributes which make God God), *did not think this equality with God was a thing to be eagerly grasped or retained; But stripped Himself* (of all privileges and rightful dignity) *so as to assume the guise of a servant* (slave), *in that He became like man and was born a human being. And after He had appeared in human form He abased and humbled Himself* (still further) *and carried His obedience to the extreme of death, even the death of* (the) *cross! Therefore* (because He stooped so low), *God has highly exalted Him and has freely bestowed on Him the name that is above every name, that in* (at) *the name of Jesus every knee should* (must) *bow, in heaven and on earth and under the earth, and every tongue* (frankly and openly) *confess and acknowledge that Jesus Christ is Lord, to the glory of God the Father."*

In Colossians 2:9 (Amplified Bible), *"For in Him* (Christ the Messiah) *the whole fullness of Deity* (the Godhead) *continues to dwell in bodily form—giving complete expression of the divine nature. And you are in Him, made full and have come to fullness of life—in Christ you too are filled with the Godhead: Father, Son and Holy Spirit, and reach full spiritual stature. And He* (Christ Messiah) *is the Head of all rule and authority."*

We are also told in Colossians 1:15-18 that *"He* (Christ Jesus the Messiah) *is the image of the invisible God, the firstborn over all creation. For by Him all things were created that are in heaven and that are on earth, visible and invisible, whether thrones or dominions or principalities or powers. All things were created by Him and for Him. And He is before all things, and in Him all things hold together. And He is the Head of the body, the church, who is the beginning, the firstborn from the dead, that in all things He may have the preeminence."*

To determine "what we must do," we must find out what God's purpose and design is for us that we might be in His will and desire for us. That we might cooperate with Him and not resist what He is working out in our daily lives ("Give us this day our daily bread"). *"For we know that all things work together for good to them* (those) *who love God, to them* (those) *who are called according to His purpose,"* (Rom. 8:28). That God has/will accomplish His purpose in and through us is stated clearly in Ephesians 3:20 (Amplified Bible), *"Now to Him Who, by the* (action of His) *power that is at work within us, is able to* (carry out His purpose and) *do super abundantly, far over and above all that we ask or think— infinitely beyond our highest prayers, desires, thoughts, hopes or dreams—To Him be glory in the church* (the body) *and in Christ Jesus throughout all generations, for ever and ever. Amen—so be it."*

We can begin to understand what God's purpose is through the following Scriptures: Ephesians 3:10, 11 (Amplified Bible), *"*(The purpose is) *that through the church* (the body of Christ) *the complicated, many sided wisdom of God in all its infinite variety and innumerable aspects might now be made known to the angelic rulers and authorities* (principalities and powers) *in the heavenly sphere. This is in accordance with the terms of the eternal and timeless purpose which He has realized and carried into effect, in* (the person of) *Christ Jesus our Lord…"* This is confirmed in Ephesians 1:22, 23 (Amplified Bible), *"He* (God) *has put all things under His* (Christ Jesus') *feet and has appointed Him* (Christ Jesus) *the universal and supreme Head of the church, which is His body, the fullness of Him Who fills it all in all—for in that body lives the full measure of Him Who makes everything complete, and Who fills everything everywhere* (with Himself)."

This body of Christ Jesus, which God has purposed, is explained and described in some wonderful detail in 1 Corinthians 12:12-27 (Amplified Bible), *"Just as the body is a unity and yet has many parts, and all the parts, though many, form* (only) *one body, so it is with Christ Jesus, the Messiah, the anointed One. For by* (means of the personal agency of) *one Holy Spirit we were all, whether Jew or Greeks, slave or free, baptized into one body, and all made to drink of one Holy Spirit. For the body does not consist of one limb or organ but of many. If the foot should say, 'Because I am not the hand, I do not belong to the body', would it therefore not be* (a part) *of the body? If the ears should say, 'Because I am not the eye, I do not belong to the body', would it therefore not be* (a part) *of the body? If the whole body were an eye, where* (would be the sense of) *hearing? If the whole body were an ear, where* (would be the sense of) *smell? But as it is, God has placed and arranged the limbs and organs in the body, each* (particular one) *of them, just as He wished and saw fit and with the best adaption. But if* (the whole) *were all a single organ, where would the body be? And now there are* (certainly) *many limbs and organs, but a single body. And the eye is not able to say to the hand, 'I have no need of you', nor again the head to the feet, 'I have no need of you'.''* [Comment: could this mean that the Head (Jesus Christ the Lord) needs the feet (the saints on earth)?] *''But instead, there is* (an absolute) *necessity for the parts of the body that are considered the more weak. And those parts of the body which are considered rather ignoble are* (the very parts) *which we invest with additional honor; and our unseemly parts and those unsuitable for exposure are treated with seemliness* (modesty and decorum), *which our more presentable parts do not require. But God has so adjusted* (mingled, harmonized and subtly proportioned the parts of the whole) *body, giving the greater honor and richer endowment to the inferior parts which lack* (apparent importance), *so that there is no division or discord or lack of adaptation* (of the parts of the body to each other), *but the members all alike have a mutual interest in and care for one another. And if one member suffers, all the parts* (share) *the suffering; if one member is honored, all members* (share in) *the enjoyment of it. Now you* (collectively) *are Christ's body and* (individually) *you are members of it, each part severally and distinct—each with his own place and function.''*

The Gospel truth that we, the body of Christ, composed of Biblical Christians, are to form ''one new man'' is stated in Ephesians 2:14-16, *''For He Himself* (Christ Jesus) *is our peace, who made both* (Hebrew and Gentile) *one, and has broken down the middle wall of division between us, having abolished in His flesh the enmity, that is, the law of commandments contained in ordinances, so as to create in Himself one new man from the two, thus making peace, and that He might reconcile them both to God in one body by the*

101

cross, by it having put to death the enmity." (Here again, clearly stated, there is *no* difference any longer to God between Jew or Gentile!)

That Biblical Christians are *"flesh of His flesh and bone of His bone"* in His body the church is found in Ephesians 5:30 and 32, *"For we are members of His body, flesh of His flesh, and bone of His bones...This is a great mystery, but I speak concerning Christ and the church."*

These Scriptures speak so clearly that no theological explanation or interpretation is needed. They tell us ever so plainly that the body of our Lord Jesus Christ is composed of Biblical Christians here on earth *today*. This body is also the church here on earth *today*. The head of this body is the Lord Jesus Christ. The individual members of His body are to be so fitly joined and united together by the power of God Himself in the manifested indwelling Holy Spirit, so as to bring forth *"one new man,"* here on earth.

Each individual member of this *"one new man"* body is of vital importance to the body as a whole. It is absolutely essential that each member perform its *ordained* function. If a member fails, the whole body suffers. This fact is at once a blessing, to be a member, yet the responsibility is humbling, in that the great purpose of God for mankind here on earth depends on how each member of the body of Christ Jesus performs its specific functions in the body. The *"one new man,"* composed of multitudes of individual Biblical Christians, will *not* be a product of man's organizations and programs, as important as they may be. The *"one new man"* shall be brought forth by the wonder-working power of the Holy Spirit and the indwelling Christ. God's plan for mankind here on earth will be accomplished, fulfilled, finished and consummated. God's plan has *not* failed and God's plan will *not* fail! Amen, so be it!

There is absolutely no way an individual Adamic man can

fulfill his/her essential, ordained function and responsibility as a member of the body of our Lord Jesus Christ without the indwelling and functioning Holy Spirit of God the Father. It is by the power of the Holy Spirit that a believer becomes a member of the body of Christ. *"For by one Holy Spirit were you baptized into the body of Christ,* (1 Corinthians 12:13).*"* *"For as many of you as have been baptized into Christ* (by the Holy Spirit) *have put on Christ. There is neither Jew nor Greek* (Gentile)*...bond* (slave) *nor free...male nor female: For ye* (you) *are all one in Christ Jesus* (Galatians 3:27, 28).*"* We are also reminded that *"The first man Adam became a living soul. The last Adam became a life giving spirit...The first man was of the earth, made of dust; the second Man is the Lord Jesus Christ from heaven,"* (1 Corinthians 15:45 and 47).

Variations of the phrase, "Holy Spirit baptism," appear many times in the Bible and it is vital and essential to the individual to fulfill his/her God ordained function as a member of the "one new man, body of Christ." Indeed, as we have just seen in 1 Corinthians 12:13, the believer is "Holy Spirit baptized into the body of Christ" to be united with other Biblical Christians in the "one new man, body of Christ."

All believers know John 3:16, but let us consider Luke 3:16 where John the baptizer was asked if he was the expected Christ (Messiah). He answers, *"I indeed baptize you with water; but One mightier* (greater) *than I cometh,* (Whose sandal strap) *I am not worthy to unloose. He shall baptize you with the Holy Spirit and with fire."* This is found also in Mark 1:8. Jesus reminds His disciples of this in Acts 1:5-8 saying, *"Wait for that which the Father has promised, which I have told you, 'That John baptized with water', but you shall be baptized with the Holy Spirit not many days from now." Jesus* continues saying, *"You will receive power when the Holy Spirit has come upon you..."* Peter recalls this promise of Jesus saying, *"I remember the words of the Lord, when He used to say 'John baptized with water, but you shall be baptized with the Holy Spirit,'"* (Acts 11:16).

It is worthwhile to notice that those whom Jesus breathed on saying, *"Receive ye the Holy Spirit,"* (John 20:22), *were among those whom* (He) *"commanded them not to depart from Jerusalem, but wait for the Promise of the Father,"* (Acts 1:4). From this fact alone, it is obvious they had not gotten the *fullness* of the Holy Spirit (Promise of the Father) when Jesus *"breathed on them."* For if they had, He would not have commanded (not an option) them to *"wait for the Promise of the Father."*

The Holy Spirit baptism (the Promise of the Father) was initially given in Acts 2:1-4, *"And when the day of Pentecost was fully come, they were all with one accord in one place. And suddenly there came a sound from heaven, as of a rushing mighty wind, and it filled all the house* (whole room) *where they were sitting. And there appeared unto them cloven* (divided) *tongues like as of fire, and it sat upon each of them. And they were all filled with the Holy Ghost* (Spirit) *and began to speak with other tongues, as the Holy Spirit gave them utterance."* Reading on, you find they were speaking languages (tongues) they had not learned, but were understood by others who spoke those languages (tongues). In passing, it is interesting to note, that there are three different types or characters of "tongues" described in Scriptures. The one type of Acts 2, which was understood by various ones present to whom that language/tongue was native or learned. Another type of "tongue" of 1 Corinthians 12:10, which, when given in a gathering of Biblical Christians is to be interpreted. Both the "tongue" and "interpretation" (not a translation) are given by the same Holy Spirit. Then there is the "tongue" which is a prayer language and is discussed in 1 Corinthians 14:2 as, *"speaketh not unto men but unto God."* In verse 14 we read, *"For if I pray in an unknown tongue, my spirit prayeth* (to God), *but my understanding is unfruitful."* And we learn in verse 4 that *"He who speaks/prays in a tongue edifies and improves himself."*

We have learned from the Scriptures that the Lord Jesus Christ is the one who baptizes with the Holy Spirit. You can search the Scriptures and you will *not* find that the giving of the gift of the Holy Spirit baptism ever ceased or ended. In fact, the Scriptures state that *"Jesus Christ* (the Holy Spirit Baptizer) *is the same yesterday* (past), *today* (present) *and forever* (future),*"* (Hebrews 13:8). Jesus says, *"Heaven and earth shall pass away, but My words shall not pass away,"* (Mark 13:31). The book, *"They Speak In Other Tongues"* by *John Sherrill*, is excellent.

What about those who say that this gift of the Holy Spirit as manifest by "speaking in tongues according to the Scriptures is of the Devil/Satan?" They should review and take heed of the words of our Lord Jesus Christ in Mark 3:29 where He issues His most severe warning saying, *"He that shall blaspheme* (speaks abusively against or maliciously misrepresents) *the Holy Ghost* (Spirit) *never* (has) *forgiveness, but is in danger of eternal condemnation."*

We might do well to review accounts of the giving and receiving of the Holy spirit baptism *after* that initial outpouring of Acts, chapter two.

Saint Paul is an excellent example. In 1 Corinthians 14:18, he says, *"I thank my God I speak with tongues more than ye all."* Paul became a believer on the road to Damascus (Acts 9:3-6) and a disciple of Jesus Christ named,

105

Ananias, was told by the Lord where to find Paul (Saul), Acts 9:10-17, Ananias went to Paul to lay hands on him saying, *"Brother Saul, the Lord, even Jesus that appeared unto thee* (on the road as you came) *hath sent me that* (you may receive your sight) *and be filled with the Holy Ghost* (Spirit)." In Acts 19:1-7, we find Saint Paul at Ephesus where he found some disciples whom he asked, *"'Did you receive the Holy Spirit since you became believers?' And they said to him, 'We have not so much as heard whether there is a Holy Spirit.' And Paul said to them, 'Into what then were you baptized?' And they said, 'Into John's baptism.' Then Paul said, 'John indeed baptized with the baptism of repentance, saying to the people that they should believe on Him who would come after him, that is, on Christ Jesus.' When they heard this they were baptized in the name of the Lord Jesus. And when Paul had laid his hands on them, the Holy Spirit came upon them, and they spoke with tongues and prophesied."*

Notice they were believers, but had *not* received the gift of the Holy Spirit baptism. This account of Paul ministering, follows the pattern outlined by Peter. After he was baptized with the Holy Spirit and had given an anointed sermon, Peter was asked by non-believers, *"'What shall we do?' Then Peter said unto them, 'Repent, and be baptized in the name of Jesus Christ for the remission of sins; and ye shall receive the gift of the Holy Ghost* (Spirit), *for the promise is unto you and to your children and to all that are afar off* (time and distance wise), *even as many as the Lord our God shall call,'"* (Acts 2:37-39).

Chapter 10 of the Book of Acts is devoted to the conversion of the Roman centurion named, Cornelius, at Caesarea, who believed in God, revered God, prayed to God, with all his family, and gave alms generously to the poor. God spoke to Cornelius and told him where Saint Peter was to be found and that Peter would tell him what he must do to receive an even greater blessing. At the same time, God was speaking to Peter (verses 1 through 16), Cornelius sent two servants and a soldier to Peter. God told Peter to go with the man to the house of Cornelius. When Cornelius worshiped Peter, Peter forbid him saying, *"Stand up; I myself am also a man."* While Peter was explaining to all present that it was *"an unlawful thing for a* (Hebrew) *to keep company* (with another race). *But God hath shewed me that I should not call any man common or unclean,"* (verses 16 through 27). While Peter was sharing the Gospel with them (verses 34 through 43), the Holy Spirit fell on all those who heard the word and Peter, *"heard them speak with tongues and magnify God,"* (verses 44 through 46). *Seeing that they had received the gift of the Holy Spirit baptism just as Peter had on the day of Pentecost, Peter, "commanded them to be* (water) *baptized in the name of the Lord Jesus,"* (verses 47, 48).

When the other disciples demanded that Peter explain why he had taken the Gospel to Gentiles, Chapter 11 of Acts relates Peter's answer. In verses 15 through 18 Peter concludes, *"And as I began to speak, the Holy Ghost* (Spirit) *fell on them, as on us at the beginning,* (Acts 2). *Then remembered I the word of the Lord, how that He said, 'John indeed baptized with water, but ye shall be baptized with the Holy Ghost* (Spirit).' (If) *then God gave them the like* (same) *gift as He* (gave) *us who believed on the Lord Jesus Christ, what was I that I could withstand* (or resist) *God? When they heard these things they* (became silent)*; and glorified God, saying, 'Then hath God also to the Gentiles granted repentance unto life.'"*

From this account we see again that the Holy Spirit baptism

107

was given to "believers" (the initial 120, then 3,000, then Paul, those at Ephesus and Cornelius' family and friends) but Cornelius et. al. received the Holy Spirit baptism *before* being water-baptized in the name of the Lord Jesus, but *after* they believed.

We find in Acts 11:26 that Paul (Saul) was brought ***"unto Antioch. And it came to pass, that a whole year they assembled themselves with the church and taught*** (many) ***people. And the disciples were called Christians first in Antioch."*** We can be very sure these disciples with Paul had received the promised gift of the Holy Spirit after they became believers and then they were recognized and identified as Christians.

Why does God fulfill His promised Holy Spirit baptism through our Lord Jesus Christ? Jesus answers this questions in Acts 1:8 (Amplified Bible)...***"You shall receive power—ability, efficiency and might—when the Holy Spirit has come upon you; and*** (then) ***you shall*** (have the power) ***to be My witnesses in Jerusalem, and all Judea and Samaria and to the ends—the very bounds—of the earth."*** Please notice the power that comes through the Holy Spirit baptism, was a power (ability) to ***"be witnesses"*** of and for our Lord Jesus Christ. As important as witnessing is—being a living witness is more effective and is the base and foundation upon which effective witnessing is built. The disciples at Antioch had this indwelling power (ability) of the Holy Spirit and were recognized and identified as Christians. Only when our lives and actions reveal and manifest the indwelling Christ by the power of the Holy Spirit, will our witness be most effective. Our calling is to *be Christ*ians.

We can see the power of the Holy Spirit baptism in the life of Saint Peter. Before Pentecost, Peter had not been a person of consistent power. He even denied that he knew Jesus Christ (Luke 22:58). After receiving the God-promised

108

Holy Spirit baptism, Peter had the power (ability) to deliver a Holy Spirit-anointed sermon which caused "about 3,000" to repent from their sins, believe on the Lord Jesus Christ, be baptized in water "in the name of Jesus Christ for the remission of sins," and "receive the gift of the Holy Spirit" baptism (Acts 2:14-38). The difference between Peter the *chicken*, and Peter the *rock*, was Pentecost! After Pentecost, Peter had the *power* (ability) to *be* a witness for Jesus Christ.

At the house of Cornelis, Peter points to the fact that Jesus received His power (ability) through the Holy Spirit when he said, *"God anointed Jesus of Nazareth with the Holy Ghost* (Spirit) *and with power,"* (Acts 10:38).

It is by the power of the Holy Spirit that we become members of the body/church of the Lord Jesus Christ, *"For by one* (Holy) *Spirit are we all baptized into one body* (of Jesus Christ),"* according to 1 Corinthians 12:13. Notice, this is accomplished through the "Holy Spirit baptism", *not* water baptism, which is *"for the remission of sins,"* (Mark 1:4, Luke 3:3 and Acts 2:38).

To be an effective Biblical Christian, actively functioning as a member of the body/church of our Lord Jesus Christ, we must be completely and totally led by the Holy Spirit. And then on to sonship: *"For as many as are led by the* (Holy) *Spirit of God, they are the sons of God,"* yes, even on to become the *"manifested* (revealed) *sons of God,"* (Romans 8:14, 19). It should be perfectly clear to all believers and Biblical Christians that the achieving of this purpose of God, to *"bring forth the one perfect man,"* the body/church of Christ Jesus cannot be done without the power of the Holy Spirit working in each individual member. Each member needs the Holy Spirit baptism. *"Are you so foolish and so senseless and so silly? Having begun* (your new life spiritually) *with the* (Holy) *Spirit, are you now reaching for perfection/completion* (by dependence) *on the flesh?"* (Gal. 3:3, Amplified Bible).

109

How does one receive the Holy Spirit baptism? First, read the second chapter of the Book of Acts in a translation you can easily understand. May I suggest a few: *The Amplified Bible, The New Internation Version* (in book format), *The New King James Bible, The New American Standard* and *The Jerusalem Bible.*

You will see in verse 38 of Acts 2, Peter tells us what we must do, **"Repent—change your views and purpose and determine to accept the will of God in your inner selves instead of rejecting it—and be baptized** (immersed) **every one of you in the name of Jesus Christ for the forgiveness of and release from your sins; and you shall receive the gift of the Holy Spirit. For the promise** (of the Holy Spirit baptism) **is to you and your children and for all that are far away..."** (Amplified Bible).

The following is a prayer I have composed from the Holy Scriptures. If you will say it out loud, even if alone, and truly believe it, you shall be saved! (Rom. 10:9):

"Heavenly Father, I know Jesus is the Son of God and I know God raised Jesus from the dead. I now proclaim that Jesus is Lord. Jesus is my Lord. Lord, have mercy on me, a sinner. Lord Jesus, I confess and acknowledge my sins. I am sorry I committed them. I ask You to forgive and remove all my sins. By Your Word I know I am forgiven of all my sins. I am washed clean by the blood You shed on the cross. I am now a new creation in Christ Jesus! All the old things are passed away—all things are now new. I accept Your forgiveness and thank You for it. I renounce and reject the Devil and all his works in my past life.

"Lord Jesus, I forgive all those who have abused, mistreated and hurt me, in the same way You have forgiven me. I ask You to bless those who have cursed me and come into their lives also.

"Lord Jesus, be Lord of my life—rule and reign in my life make me what You would have me to be. I thank You, Lord Jesus. Amen!"

You are now "saved", as it is written, "That whosoever (just anyone) shall call upon the name of the Lord (Jesus) shall be saved," (Acts 2:21 and Rom. 10:13). You are now a "believer!"

To follow the sequence of the pattern outlined in Acts 2:38, you would now be baptized in water as a public acclamation that you have accepted Jesus as your Lord and Savior. To also acknowledge His forgiveness of your sins, (Acts 2:38) and as a representation that you are, **"Buried with Him** (Jesus Christ) **in baptism, wherein also ye are risen with Him through the faith of the operation** (working) **of God, Who hath raised Him** (Jesus) **from the dead,"** (Col. 2:12).

However, we know that God is sovereign and paramount to do as He wants, to accomplish His promises and purposes, but being faithful to His word. We know from Acts 10:44-48, that the believers gathered at Cornelius' house were baptized in the Holy Spirit *before* they were baptized in water.

In Luke 11:10 Jesus tells us, ***"Everyone who asks receives, and he who seeks finds, and to him who knocks it shall be opened. If a son asks for bread from any of you who are a father, will you give him a stone? Or if he asks for a fish, will you give him a serpent instead of a fish? Or if he asked for an egg, will you offer him a scorpion? If you then, being evil, know how to give good gifts to your children, how much more will your heavenly Father give the Holy Spirit to those who ask Him."*** Ask the Lord Jesus Christ to baptize you in His Holy Spirit.

After the initial one hundred twenty who received the Holy Spirit baptism on the morning of Pentecost, most believers received this blessed gift by the laying on of hands by someone who had previously received the Holy Spirit baptism. Peter and John were sent to Samaria and there ***"they laid their hands on*** (the believers)***, and they received the Holy Ghost*** (Spirit)***,"*** (Acts 8:17). And remember Ananias ***"put his hands on him Paul*** (Saul)***...to be filled with the Holy Ghost*** (Spirit)***,"*** (Acts 9:17). Then later Paul went to Ephesus where he found twelve believers. ***"And when Paul laid his hands upon them, the Holy Ghost*** (Spirit) ***came on them, and they spake with other tongues and prophesied,"*** (Acts 19:6).

With the current outpouring of this blessed and promised Holy Spirit baptism, it should not be at all difficult to find individuals, congregations, prayer groups, Bible study groups or a *Full Gospel Business Mens' Fellowship* chapter where this Biblical laying-on-of-hands is practiced. Just remember that the Lord Jesus Christ is the *only* Holy Spirit baptizer—not men or women. An excellent book is *"To Receive The Holy Spirit"* by *Gerald Derstine, Rt. 2, Box 279, Bradenton,*

FL 34202.

After we have received the gift of the Holy Spirit baptism—we have not arrived—we do not have it all—but we have more than when we first believed. God is not through with us yet, no matter how much we speak in other tongues, prophecy or manifest the other gifts of the Holy Spirit listed in 1 Corinthians 12. However, if you believe you have all God has for you, then your pilgrimage is over. Because once you have arrived, the journey has ended. However, you would do well to review the words of our Lord Jesus in Mark 7:22, to see what He lists along with, "pride."

Hebrew Feasts and Holy Days

To find out what is available to the Biblical Christians who want to obtain and attain all the blessing that God has for us, the Hebrew feasts may give some insight and understanding. Colossians 2:16, 17 states, **"Therefore let no one judge you by what you eat or drink or regarding a festival** (or holy day) **or of the new moon or of the sabbath days: Which are a shadow** (type or outline) **of things to come; but the body is of Christ."** There are certain religions which believe that Christians *must* observe such Jewish rituals, even today, however, they would do well to read this scripture and many others which *clearly* state otherwise.

As the Hebrew Feasts of Israel are prophetic (types and shadows of things to come), we would do well to review them, with that understanding in mind; as examples of what God *has* done, and how they relate to what he *is* doing and *will* do.

The three Feasts of Israel's annual cycle of religious ceremonies were: 1) The Feast of the Passover (in the first Hebrew month), 2) The Feast of Pentecost (in the third Hebrew month) and 3) The Feast of Tabernacles or Booths

113

(in the seventh Hebrew month).

These three Feasts include seven major events, three are included in the Feast of the Passover. The Feast of Pentecost is a single event. The Feast of Tabernacles/Booths is composed of three.

The following outline of the Feasts and festivals may give a better understanding:

I. **The Feast of the Passover,** or **Feast of Unleavened Bread** includes: **1)** The Passover (Exodus 12:1-23; Leviticus 23:4, 5; Deuteronomy 16:1-8). (Accepting Jesus as Savior) **2)** The Unleavened Bread (Exodus 12:18; 23:15; Leviticus 23:6-8; Deuteronomy 16:3, 4). (Removal of sin from our lives) **3)** The Sheaf of Firstfruits (Leviticus 23:10-14). (We are now new fruit-presentable to God!)

II. **The Feast of Pentecost**, or **Feast of Weeks**, or **Harvest of Firstfruits** (Exodus 23:16; Leviticus 23:15-21; Deuteronomy 16:9-12; Acts 2:1). (We now have power to live victoriously!)

III. **The Feast of Tabernacles**, or **Feast of Booths**, or **Feast of Ingatherings** includes: **1)** The Blowing of Trumpets (Leviticus 23:24, 25) (Announcing the second coming) **2)** The Day of Atonement, or Yom Kippur (Leviticus 16:29-34; 23:27-32). (All men are judged at the second coming) **3)** The Feast of Tabernacles (Exodus 23:16; Leviticus 23:34-44; Deuteronomy 16:13-15). (Believers can praise and worship God forever!)

From the Scriptures we find that the Feast of the Passover is on the fourteenth day of the first Hebrew month and the fifteenth day is the Feast of Unleavened Bread. Both of these consecutive Feast days are Sabbath days ("you shall do no servile work"). The Feast of Pentecost is a Sabbath day. The Blowing of Trumpets (first day of the seventh month) is a Sabbath day. The Day of Atonement, or Yom Kippur (tenth day of the seventh month) is a Sabbath day. The Feast of Tabernacles starts on the fifteenth day of the seventh month and lasts seven days, with the first day being a Sabbath day. The day after the last day of the Feast of Tabernacles is a Sabbath, for a total of seven Sabbaths. These designated Sabbath days are Sabbath (no work) days regardless of what day of the week they might fall upon. Not understanding this fact may account for the celebration of "Good Friday" as the crucifixion day of our Lord Jesus Christ with the following Sunday as His resurrection day. According to Scripture, this cannot be so. Remember, Jesus said He would be *"(in the earth) for three days and three nights,"* (Matt. 12:40). The women and, later, the men, found the tomb empty Sunday (the first day of the week) morning (Matt. 28:1 and Mark 16:1), for a total of only two nights (Friday and Saturday) and one day (Saturday).

This error in Christian tradition may be based on the Scriptures that say Jesus' body was placed in the tomb *"the day before the Sabbath,"* (Mark 15:42), and they found the tomb empty, *"when the Sabbath was past,"* (Mark 16:1). And in Matthew 28:1, *"After the Sabbath, as the first day of the week began to dawn..."* The originators of this "Good Friday" tradition may have thought the "Sabbath" referred to was the same Sabbath, and they assumed it was the Hebrews usual or standard Sabbath—to us, Saturday, or the last day of the week.

In Matthew 27:62; Mark 15:42; Luke 23:54 and John 19:14, 31, 42, from the Amplified Bible, we find Jesus was crucified on the Day of Preparation, which is the day before the Day of Passover, which is a Sabbath day regardless of the day of the week it happens to be. (Note: One Hebrew day ends and another day begins at sundown. We should remember the Scriptures do not say Jesus was resurrected on the first day of the week [Sunday]—only that His tomb was found empty *"as the day began to dawn."* We should also remember that faithful Hebrews could not have traveled to the tomb on any one of these Sabbath days because it was/is forbidden, (Lev.23:3). So the tomb *could have* been empty before Sunday, the first day of the week.

With this understanding of Sabbath days, we can see there could have been *three consecutive* Sabbath days immediately before the day we call Sunday—that is, before sundown on the weekly Sabbath (Sabbot) we call, Saturday, which would mark/establish the end of the last day of the week and the beginning of the first day of the week. These Sabbaths were Passover, Unleavened Bread and Sabbot (the weekly Sabbath).

Should we be celebrating, "Good Wednesday," or, "Good Thursday," instead of, "Good Friday," as the crucifixion day of our Lord Jesus Christ? Which ever you select, please do not celebrate it as *"Easter,"* which is recognizing the *Babylonian god, Ester*, the god of fertility ...rabbits and eggs...the correct name of the season is, *Passover.*

How do these prophetic Hebrew Feasts relate to us as the body/church of the Lord Jesus Christ?

These Feasts were prophetic in the life of Jesus and He is our example. Therefore, we can gain some insight into God's plan for us in the pattern of these Feasts, by looking at the pattern of the Feasts of Israel in the life of our Lord Jesus Christ.

Many readers of this may already know of the possible "big picture" of God's plan for mankind here on earth, which is as follows:

It was two thousand (2,000) years from Adam to Abraham, and two thousand (2,000) years from Abraham to Jesus, and another two thousand (2,000) years to the one thousand (1,000) year "millennium") of Revelation 20. We are told in Psalm 90:4 and 2 Peter 3:8 that *"a thousand years with the Lord is but one day."* So, two thousand (2,000) years would be two (2) days. Thus, the total of *"days"* here is *seven*.

This seven day pattern of God's plan for man on earth is

116

outlined in six (6) days of creation and the seventh (7th) day of rest, yes, a *Sabbath* rest. **"For He spake in a certain place** (Gen. 2:2) **'And God did rest the seventh day from all His works'...There remaineth** (yet to come) **a** (Sabbath) **rest for the people of God,"** (Heb. 4:4, 9). It is apparent (according to these terms) that nearly six thousand (6,000) years, or six (6) days have passed since Adam and the "seventh" one thousand (1,000) year/day of Sabbath rest is very near. Other "seventh day" Scriptures are: Genesis 2:1-3; Exodus 20:11 and 31:17.

There are also some "third day" Scriptures, such as: Exodus 19:10-17; Luke 13:32; John 2:1, which portray the assurance of Hosea 6:2, **"After two days** (or 2,000 years) **will He** (God) **revive us** (give us life)**; in the third day will he raise us up to live in His sight."** If we start from the birth of Jesus, two thousand (2,000) years, or two days are very near their end and the third day millennium is near.

Please notice that the "seventh day" and the "third day" are the *same day*! That is, the millennium Sabbath day of rest.

Have you ever wondered if there was any prophetic significance to Jesus waiting until Lazarus had been dead *four* days before giving life to him, (John 11:17, 39)? When Jesus told them to open the tomb, Lazarus' sister, Mary, said, **"Lord, he has been dead four days and there is a stench,** (he stinks).**"** Remember, it was four thousand years or "four days" from Adam to Jesus and, without a Savior, mankind stunk! (stinketh: King James Version).

This is also in the prophetic Hebrew Feast of the Passover as outlined in Exodus 12:2-8, the coming out of Egypt **"shall be unto you the beginning of months; it shall be the first month of the year to you. Speak ye unto all the congregation of Israel saying, 'In the tenth day of this month they shall take to them every man a** (perfect) **lamb,...take it out from** (keep it) **from the sheep, or from the goats until the fourteenth day of** *this same month...kill it in the evening.'''* From the tenth to the fourteenth day is four days. God withheld Jesus the Savior from mankind (the sheep and goats) four days (4,000 years from Abraham to Jesus) and Jesus, the perfect Lamb, was killed on the evening of the *fourteenth* day of the first Hebrew month, which is Passover.

Verses 7 and 8 of Exodus 12, foretell the power of the Lamb's blood to save and institute the Passover meal (supper), which became our Holy Communion.

Jesus was crucified during the Passover and the promised Holy Spirit baptism was initiated on the day of Pentecost; **"When the day of Pentecost was fully come..."**(Acts 2:1), but what is the prophetic significance of the Feast of Tabernacles in the life of Jesus, and therefore, in the lives of Biblical Christians?

A clue may well be in the transformation/transfiguration/change (the same Greek word is translated into these three) of Jesus, before His crucifixion, as recorded in Matthew 17:1-8; Mark 9:2-8 and Luke 9:28-36, **"Jesus took Peter, James and John out of Jerusalem** (during a Feast time)**, up to an high mountain and He was transfigured before their eyes; His face shone as the sun, His clothes were white as light. On His one hand appeared Moses, on the other Elijah. A cloud came down and covered them. A voice from the cloud said 'This is My Beloved Son, hear Him!' When the cloud lifted they saw only Jesus. Peter said, 'Lord, it is good for us to be here; Let us build three tabernacles/booths, one for You, one for Elijah and one for Moses.'''**

God speaks to us clearly through this event. Moses represents the five books of the Law, and Elijah represents the Prophets. God is telling us that we have had the Law and the Prophets, but now you have **"My Beloved Son, hear Him."** In the first verses of Hebrews, we are told that

118

"God, who at various times and different ways spoke in times past to the fathers by the prophets, has in these last days spoken to us by His Son..." So, if you are interested in prophecy, pay extra attention to the words of our Lord Jesus Christ, but the events of His life are also prophetic for us as individuals.

It is very doubtful that Peter would have suggested the making of three "tabernacles/booths or tents" except during the Feast of Tabernacles. *"Ye shall dwell in booths* (tents/shelters) *seven days...that your generations may know that I made the children of Israel to dwell in booths* (in the wilderness) *when I brought them out of the land of Egypt: I am the Lord your God,"* (Lev. 23:42, 43).

From this we see that Jesus was transformed/transfigured/changed during the Feast of Tabernacles. Therefore, those who are *"alive and remain"* unto the coming of Jesus Christ may be transformed/transfigured/changed also during the Feast of Tabernacles. Recall 1 Corinthians 15:51, 52; and 1 Thessalonians 4:15-18, and the many "redemption" of our physical body Scriptures.

There may be a more specific time prophesy in the Feast of Tabernacles. Jesus tells us that at the time *"of the coming of the Son of Man, it will be as in the days of Noah,"* (Matt. 24:37).

Remember, the Feast of Tabernacles was the seventh and last Feast. It comes in the seventh Hebrew month, includes seven days, and Noah and his family entered the ark seven days before the flood (Gen. 7:10). In Bible numerics, the number seven is associated with spiritual perfection, completeness and fullness.

The flood started on the seventeenth day of the second month (Gen. 7:11). The ark came to rest on Mount Ararat on the seventeenth day of the seventh month (Gen. 8:4). The first day of the Feast of Tabernacles is the fifteenth day of the seventh month—so the ark came to rest on Mount Ararat on the third day of the Feast of Tabernacles. Jesus said at the coming of the Son of Man it would be as in the days of Noah, (Matthew 24:37 and Luke 17:26).

Matthew 17:1 and Mark 9:2 tell us that Jesus was transfigured/transformed/changed *"after the sixth day"* and Luke 9:28 says it was *"before the eighth day,"* making it the seventh day.

If the first day of this seventh day period was the Day of Atonement/Yom Kippur, which is on the tenth day of the seventh month, then our Lord Jesus Christ was transformed/transfigured/changed on the seventeenth day of the seventh month—the *third* day of the Feast of Tabernacles.

Could the following be the prophetic pattern of the Feasts for the Biblical Christians?

If you have accepted *Jesus as your Savior*, your *spirit* has been justified, you have kept *Passover*.

If your *soul* is being sanctified by the power of the *Holy Spirit* baptism, you are in the process of keeping *Pentecost*.

Then the final part of a complete/perfect salvation will be the redemption/glorification/transformation of *your body* during the *Feast of Tabernacles*, at the *second coming*!

This pattern is confirmed in the wilderness tabernacle described in complete detail to Moses by God:

The Outer Court is a very large area, representing the great number of people who will accept Jesus as Savior. They are exposed to natural light, but half their day is darkness.

The Holy Place is a lot smaller (10 x 10 x 20 = 2,000 cubed cubits—2,000 years is a Biblical age), and is an enclosed area where the only light is from the oil of the lamp stand. Oil represents the Holy Spirit, and a smaller number of Christians are *filled* with the Holy Spirit.

The Holy of Holies or Most Holy Place, is half the size of the Holy Place (10 x 10 x 10 = 1,000 cubed cubits—the 1,000 year millennium) and the only light there is God

Himself—the Glory of His presence as in the New Jerusalem of Revelation 21:3 and 23. Volumes have been written and more, no doubt, could be written on the significance of Moses' tabernacle, but it is possibly symbolic of the number of those chosen to go *through* the tribulation *with* God, and/or those who will reign forever with Him!

To receive the fullness of God's grace and blessing, we must keep *all* the Holy Feasts. Do not stop short, but heed the exortation of Hebrews 6:1. *"...Let us go onto perfection/completeness."*

Let 1 Thessalonians 5:23, 24 be our prayer:

"May the God of peace Himself sanctify you completely; and may your whole spirit, soul and body be preserved blameless at the coming of our Lord Jesus Christ. He who calls you is faithful, He also will do it." Also Philippians 1:6, *"Being confident of this very thing, that He which hath begun a good work in you will perform* (complete) *it until the day of Jesus Christ."*

How do we keep the Feast of Tabernacles? I do not know, (yet it seems likely this is the "harvest" at the second coming). However, it is clear from Scriptures and the order of progression of the Feasts that they are to be kept in their order: *Passover* (spirit salvation) in the first month, *Pentecost* (soul salvation) in the third month, *Tabernacles* (body salvation) in the seventh month. It is well to note where the Feasts were instituted: Passover in Egypt as slaves; Pentecost in the wilderness, but free; Tabernacles in the promised land and at the time of harvest...*"the harvest is the end of the age,"* (Matt. 13:39).

If you have kept Passover (Jesus as Savior), and are keeping Pentecost (putting on the mind of Christ, through the Holy Spirit); then (and only then) are you a candidate for Tabernacles (redemption of the body by the power of the Lord). The following tabulation confirms this sequential progressing:

Jesus/man	Christ/resurrected	Lord/eternal man
Passover	Pentecost	Tabernacles
Spirit	Soul	Body
Justified	Sanctified	Glorified
Righteousness	Peace	Joy
30 Fold	60 Fold	100 Fold
The Way	The Truth	The Life
Outer Court	Holy Place	Holy of Holies
Faith	Hope	Love
Jesus/New Life	Holy Spirit/ Powerful Life	God/Glorified Life

Note: *There are many more that could be added to this list.*

Maybe we are not expected to know the exact details of how the Feast of Tabernacles will be fulfilled in our individual lives. The one hundred twenty who received the initial outpouring of the Holy Spirit through a Holy Spirit baptism, did not know nor understand what was to happen. But, they were *obedient* to the command of their Lord Jesus Christ...**"not to depart from Jerusalem, but wait for the Promise of the Father, which ye have heard of** (from) **Me; for John truly baptized with water, but ye shall be baptized with the Holy Ghost** (Spirit) **not many days hence** (from now) (Acts 1:4, 5)." When that "Promise of the Father" was fulfilled, they recognized what had happened. Peter said, **"This is that which was spoken by the prophet, Joel,"** (Acts 2:16).

When God has fulfilled his Tabernacles promise, it can be said, "This is what was spoken by the apostles of our

Lord Jesus Christ.''

This complete three-fold salvation is the *will of God* and it shall be accomplished through His love and grace in His obedient ones; ''Grace'': The desire and power to do God's will.

"Thy kingdom come Thy will be done..." Amen, so be it!

10

Blinding Doctrines Of Today

On the day the women and the disciples of Jesus had found His tomb empty, two of His disciples were walking on the road to Emmaus *"...which was about seven miles from Jerusalem. And they talked together of all these things which had happened. And so it was, while they conversed together and reasoned, that Jesus Himself drew near and went with them. But their eyes were restrained, so that they did not know Him. And He said to them, 'What manner of conversation is this that you have with one another as you walk and are sad?' And the one whose name was Cleopas answered and said to Him, 'Are you a stranger in Jerusalem, and have You not known the things which have happened there in these days?' And He said to them, 'What things?' And they answered Him, 'Concerning Jesus of Nazareth, who was a Prophet mighty in deed and word before God and all the people, and how the chief priests and our rulers delivered Him to be condemned to death, and have crucified Him. But we were hoping that it was He who was going to redeem Israel. And besides all this, today is the third day since these things happened. Yes, and certain women of our company, who were at the tomb early, astonished us. And when they did not find His body, they came saying that they had also seen a vision of angels who said He was alive. And certain of those* (men) *who were with us went to the tomb and found it just as the women had said; but Him they did not see.' Then Jesus said unto them, 'Oh, foolish ones, and slow of heart to believe all that the prophets have spoken! Ought not the Christ to have suffered these things and to have entered into His glory?' And* **beginning at Moses and all the Prophets,** *He expounded to them* **in all the Scriptures the things concerning Himself''** (Luke 24:13-27, NKJ). Wouldn't it be wonderful to have a video or audio cassette tape of Jesus expounding to them?

Much can be learned from this ''on the road to Emmaus'' Scripture, but our discussion will be to show how false doctrines can blind us to the point that we would not recognize our Lord Jesus Christ if He walked right beside us here on earth! If men who actually *saw* and *heard Jesus* could be so deceived, it is more than a possibility that many Christians are being deceived today, no matter how *sincere* they may be.

To digress a moment: Years ago, reading this passage of Scripture, I was saddened with the thought that if two of Jesus' disciples could not recognize Him as He walked beside them, what hope could I have of recognizing Him because I had never seen Him as they had. Then a thought (I believe it was God-given) came to me, ''Remember Saint Thomas!'' I did.

We may recall Thomas was not present the first time Jesus appeared to His other disciples. When these disciples told

125

Thomas, *"he said to them, 'Unless I see in His hands the print of the nails, put my finger into the print of the nails and put my hands into His side, I will not believe.' After eight days His disciples were again inside, and Thomas was with them. Jesus came, the doors being shut, and stood in the midst and said, 'Peace be with you* (Shalom).' *Then He said to Thomas, 'Reach your finger here, and look at My hands; and reach your hand here, and put it into My side. And do not be unbelieving, but believing.' And Thomas answered and said to Him, 'My Lord and my God.' Jesus said to him, 'Thomas, because you have seen Me, you have believed. Blessed are those who have not seen and yet have believed,'"* (John 20:25-29, NKJ).

First, you *"who have not seen* (Jesus) *and yet have believed"* are just as blessed as Saint Thomas!

Second, Jesus tells us, *"For many shall come in My name, saying, 'I am Christ,' and shall deceive many,"* (Matthew 24:4, 5).

So, if someone comes to you saying, "I am the Christ," shake hands with him and check for holes or scars! How is that for the simplicity of the Gospel?!

Back "on the road to Emmaus" after that detour!

The erroneous, false doctrines of the religious leaders of those days were many, just like today. But the one the disciples had accepted was, "when the Messiah comes, He will re-establish the geographical, political nation of Israel." Israel had ceased to be a nation when conquered by Nebuchadnezzar about 588 BC. They could see in the Scriptures there would again be a nation (Isa. 1:26; Ezek. 37:11-14; Amos 9:14, 15). Israel became a nation 14 May 1948.

Jesus Himself had repeatedly told them before his crucifixion that He would be betrayed into the hands of men who would kill Him, but after three days and three nights, He would be resurrected (Matt. 16:21, 17:22, 20:17-19; Mark 8:31, 9:31; and Luke 9:22, 18:31-33). The betrayal and death of our Lord Jesus Christ was also prophesied repeatedly in the Old Testament, but they chose to ignore those Scriptures (like so many people today) and selected those Scriptures that would resolve their immediate situation—get the Romans out of Israel!

The fact that it was commonly and generally understood the coming Messiah would be the King (ruler) of Israel (the Jews) is established in the following Scriptures:

"After Jesus was born in Bethlehem of Judea (see Micah 5:2) *in the days of Herod the King, behold, wise men of the East came to Jerusalem, saying, 'Where is He who has been born King of the Jews? For we have seen His star in the east and have come to worship Him!' When Herod the king heard these things, he was troubled, and all of Jerusalem with him"* (Matt. 2:1-3, NKJ). Herod asked the wise men of the East "what time the star appeared" and to let him know when they had found the Child. They found the Child, but did not tell Herod. The Lord God appeared to Joseph in a dream saying, *"Arise, take the young child and His mother, flee into Egypt, and stay there until I bring you word; for Herod will seek the young Child to destroy Him."* They fled to Egypt and Herod *"put to death all the male children from two years old and under, according to the time which he had determined the wise men had first seen the star,"* (Matt. 2:10-16). Clearly Herod feared that Jesus would become king/ruler of Israel. Some thirty-three years later at His mock trial, Pilate asked the crowd, *"do you want me to release to you the King of the Jews?"* (John 18:39) And the soldiers mocked Jesus saying, *"Hail, King of the Jews"* (John 19:3). When Jesus hung upon the cross, they put the sign over His head on which Herod had written in Hebrew, Greek and Latin, *"Jesus of Nazareth, the King of the Jews,"*

(John 19:19).

Even the disciples of Jesus had become victims of this deception in spite of all the many times He had told them of His death and resurrection. We read in Matthew 20:20, 21 and Mark 10:37, the mother of the sons of Zebedee (James and John) came to Jesus with her sons, kneeling down and asking something from Him. *"And he said to her, 'What do you wish?' She said to Him, 'Grant that these two sons of mine may sit one on Your right hand and the other on the left, in Your kingdom/rule.'"* In Mark 9:34 and 10:37, His disciples *"disputed among themselves, who should be the greatest."*

Even after His crucifixion, resurrection and appearances to His disciples, they still clung to the false doctrine that He would establish the nation of Israel with Him as its King. In Acts 1:6, just before His return to the Father, the last question His disciples asked Him was, *"Lord, wilt Thou at this time restore again* (establish) *the kingdom* (nation) *of Israel?"*

Back to the two disciples, "on the road to Emmaus" explaining to Jesus they all were sure Jesus was the Messiah, but must not have been the expected Messiah because, *"He did not redeem* (re-establish) *the nation of Israel."* And this false doctrine so blinded them that they did not recognize the Lord Jesus Christ walking along with them!

There are many similar, blinding, false doctrines today. We will explore a few of them in light of the whole council of God's Word, with the hope of opening a few eyes to *"be established in the present truth"* (2 Peter 1:12).

These doctrines are like the *theory* of evolution—they start as a theory or hypothesis which is often repeated, without serious questioning, until it is accepted as fact or truth or doctrine.

First, let us explore the "Seventy Weeks (Sevens) of Daniel." There are quite a few erroneous theories based on

128

interpretations of Daniel 9, in many Christian circles, that have become doctrines. One of those is that there is a so-called, *"gap,"* between the sixty-ninth and seventieth weeks. This, *"gap,"* is accepted to be about two thousand years, at the end of which, Jesus is to return.

In passing, it is interesting that Jesus referred to this prophet by name in Matthew 24:15...*"spoken of by Daniel the prophet,"* but is doubtful that Jesus was referring to a *"gap"* in Daniel 9.

"In the first year of his reign (of Darius), *I, Daniel, understood from the Scriptures, according to the Word of the Lord given to Jeremiah the prophet,* (Jer. 5:11, 12 and 29:10), *that the desolation of Jerusalem would last seventy years,"* (verse 2, NIV).

Darius, the Mede, became King of Babylon in 538 BC.

"So I turned to the Lord God, and pleaded with Him in prayer and petition (supplications), *in fasting, and in sackcloth, and ashes."* (verse 3). And *"while I was speaking and praying, confessing my sin, and the sin of my people Israel, and making my request to the Lord my God..."* (verse 20, NIV), God's special messenger, Gabriel, came upon Daniel (Luke 1:19, Gabriel spoke to Zacharias, father of John the baptizer and in Luke 1:26-37, Gabriel spoke to Mary about her bringing forth the Son of God) saying, *"Daniel, I have now come to give to you insight and understanding* (of the vision)... *seventy* (weeks) (literally, "seventy units of seven") *are decreed for your people and your holy city* (Jerusalem), *to finish transgression, to put an end to sin, to atone for wickedness, to bring in everlasting righteousness, to seal up* (complete) *vision and prophecy, and to anoint the Most Holy. Know and understand this: From the issuing of the decree to restore and rebuild Jerusalem until the Anointed One* (Messiah the Prince)...*will be seven 'sevens'* (weeks) (units of seven) *and sixty two 'sevens'*

(weeks)'' (units of seven) (a total of 69): (the street and wall shall be built again even in troubled times,) (Dan. 9:22-25, NIV).

There can be no doubt that these verses were prophetic as to how long Jerusalem would be desolate and the coming of ''Messiah the Prince'' and would be accomplished within sixty-nine weeks (units of seven). However, the fulfillment of the seven divine purposes and objectives of verse 24 would be accomplished in the seventieth week (unit of sevens). ''Messiah the Prince'' would fulfill the seven prophesied divine objectives:

1. *"To finish transgression."* In Hebrews 10:12 and 14 we read, *"This Man* (Jesus)*, after He had offered one sacrifice for **transgressions** and sin forever, sat down at the right hand of God...For by one offering He has perfected forever them that are sanctified."*

2. *"To put an end to sin."* *"...Jesus came **to put an end to sin** by the sacrifice of Himself"* (Heb. 9:26b). *"Behold the Lamb of God, which taketh away the sin of the world,"* (John 1:29).

3. *"To atone* (make reconciliation) **for wickedness** (iniquities)."* *"Their sins and **iniquities** will I* (God) *remember no more,"* (Heb. 10:17). And in 2 Corinthians 5:18, *"God was in Christ* (Jesus) **reconciling** the world to Himself."*

4. *"To bring in everlasting righteousness."* We are assured in 1 Corinthians 1:30, *"...(You are) in Christ Jesus, who of God is made unto us wisdom and **righteousness**..."* And in 2 Corinthians 5:21, *"For He hath* (God) *made Him* (Jesus) *to be sin for us, who knew no sin; that we might be made the **righteousness** of God in Jesus Christ."*

5. *"To seal up* (complete) **vision**."* In Acts 26:17-19 Saint Paul refers to his assignment, by Jesus Christ the Lord, to take the Gospel to the Gentiles as *"the heavenly*

vision.'' Remember, *"God so loved the world, that He gave His only begotten Son* (for the sin of the world),*"* (John 3:16).

6. *"And* (seal up/complete) **prophecy.*'* The Lord Jesus Christ declares, *"I came to **fulfill and complete the law and prophecy,*'* (Matt. 5:17).

7. *"To anoint the Most High.*'* The word, "Christ," literally means God's Anointed; "Christ Jesus", the Anointed Savior. In Luke 4:16-21, Jesus stood up in the synagogue in Nazareth on the Sabbath day and read Isaiah 61:1 and 2, *"The Spirit of the Lord is upon Me, because He hath **anointed Me** to preach the Gospel to the poor. He hath sent Me to heal the brokenhearted, to preach deliverance to the captives and recovering of sight to the blind, to set at liberty those that are bruised* (oppressed), *to preach the acceptable year of the Lord.''* ...He closed the Book and said to all of them, *"This day is this Scripture fulfilled in your ears.''*

It is possible that Jesus was referring to these seven purposes and objectives, and more when He spoke His last words from the cross, *"It is finished/*completed.''

Picking up again at verse 26 of Daniel, *"And **after the sixty-two weeks** (units of seven) (remember, there are seven units of seven before this sixty-two weeks [units of seven], making a total of sixty-nine weeks [units of seven] or in the seventieth) *shall Messiah the Prince be cut off* (killed or crucified) *but not for Himself. And the people* (troops) *of the prince* (ruler) *who is to come* (after the seventieth week) (unit of seven) *will destroy the city* (Jerusalem) *and the sanctuary/temple. And its end will come with an overflowing (of troops); even to the end, war will be decreed for desolations/destructions.''* The statements contained within the brackets are parenthetical statements, giving information in addition to the primary subject, which is, "Messiah the Prince."

131

We all know that our Lord Jesus Christ was crucified or, "cut off," as specifically prophesied in Isaiah 53:8 and confirmed/accomplished in Matthew 27:35, Mark 15:25, Luke 23:33 and John 19:18.

We also know Jesus prophesied the temple would be destroyed again in Matthew 24:1, 2; Mark 13:1, 2 and Luke 21:5, 6 where we read, *"And Jesus came out from the temple and was going away when His disciples came up to point out the temple buildings to Him. Jesus said to them, 'Do you see all these things? Truly I say to you, not one stone here shall be left upon another, which will not be torn down.'"*

According to the historian, Flavius Josephus, who was born 37AD and died sometime after 100AD, tells us that Caesar Titus conquered Jerusalem with a large army and destroyed the temple 70AD. We will show that this was, "after the seventieth week (unit of sevens)."

From history it is obvious that the "units of seven" or "weeks" refers to seven years. However, if you prefer the King James Version term, "weeks," then look at Genesis 29:27 which says, *"Fulfill her week, and we will give thee this also for the service which thou shalt serve with me yet seven other years."* And in Ezekiel 4:6, *"...I have appointed thee each day for a year."*

These last four verses of chapter 9 of the Book of Daniel are devoted to the time of "Messiah the Prince," which is the Lord Jesus Christ, or God's Anointed One. With the knowledge that this term "seventy weeks (units of seven)" was actually four hundred ninety (490) years (70 x 7), they could have calculated the exact year Messiah the Prince would appear and be manifested/revealed. This long awaited and often prophesied event was to occur at the end/completion of four hundred eighty three (483) years from the completion of seventy years of the desolation of Jerusalem. That is at the end of seven weeks (units of seven) plus sixty-two weeks (units of seven), $7(7 + 62) = 7 \times 69 = 483$ years, after 70 years of the desolation of Jerusalem.

Several kings issued "commandments" and decrees to "build again Jerusalem," but it remained for a decree of Artaxerxes (Art-a-zerk-zees) to accomplish the fulfillment of this promise of God delivered by Gabriel to Daniel who recorded for all to read.

Let us calculate with the "seventy weeks (units of seven)" as Daniel had done on the *"seventy years in the desolations of Jerusalem* (Daniel 9:2).*"*Daniel 9:25, *"...From the going forth of the commandment* (or decree) *to build* (again) *Jerusalem unto Messiah the Prince shall be 7 weeks* (units of sevens) *and 62 weeks* (units of sevens).*"*

$$
\begin{array}{lll}
7 \text{ units of seven} = & 7 \times 7 = & 49 \text{ years} \\
+62 \text{ units of seven} = & +7 \times 62 = & +434 \text{ years} \\
\hline
69 \text{ units of seven} = & 7 \times 69 = & 483 \text{ years (unto Messiah} \\
& & \text{the Prince)} \\
& & - 458 \text{ BC (Artaxerxes'} \\
& & \text{first decree)} \\
\hline
& & = 25 \text{ AD} \\
& & + 1 \\
\hline
& & = 26 \text{ AD (Messiah the} \\
& & \text{Prince to be} \\
& & \text{revealed.)}
\end{array}
$$

One year must be added when going from BC to AD.

To determine exactly when Messiah the Prince was revealed, or manifested, we can do some more calculating from numbers given in Luke 3:1, 21-23, *"Now in the fifteenth year of the reign of Tiberius Caesar...it came to pass that Jesus* (Messiah the Prince) *also being baptized; and while He prayed, the heaven was opened. And the Holy Ghost* (Spirit) *descended in a bodily shape like a dove upon Him, and a voice came from heaven which said,*

'Thou art My beloved Son; in Thee I am well pleased.'
And Jesus Himself began to be (was) *about thirty years*
of age..."

11AD Tiberius Caesar began his reign
+15AD Jesus was baptized "in the 15th year of His reign"
26AD Messiah the Prince *was* revealed!

This can also be confirmed with a different starting point
for the calculations. Remember, the *"seventy weeks* (units
of seven)*"* (490 years) were to start when the *"seventy year
desolation of Jerusalem"* ended. Desolate means no people in that land, void, vacant, empty, blank, barren and devoid
of people. The key word in these calculations is,
"desolate/desolation of Jerusalem," as in Jeremiah 25:11,
II Chronicles 36:21 and Daniel 9:2.

In a book, *God's Plan For The Ages* by *Gordon Lindsay,*
founder of Christ For The Nations Bible School, Dallas,
Texas, Lindsay calculated it took sixty years to remove all
the people from Jerusalem to Babylon—until Jerusalem was
desolate.

588 BC, Nebuchadnezzar, King of Babylon conquered
Israel/Jerusalem
− 60 years to render Jerusalem *desolate*
= 528 BC Jerusalem is made *desolate*
− 70 years Jerusalem is completely desolate
= 458 BC End of Babylonian captivity—Beginning of the 490
years (70 weeks)
− 483 years (7 weeks + 62 weeks = 69 weeks = 483 years
unto Messiah the Prince
= 25 AD
+ 1 year when passing from BC to AD
= 26 AD Messiah the Prince (Jesus) *was* revealed/manifested!

134

Now we can understand why Jesus said to the Pharisees and Sadducees, *"Oh, ye hypocrites,...but can ye not discern or recognize the signs of the times?"* (Matthew 16:3).

Back to Daniel 9:26, 27, *"After the threescore and two* (sixty-two weeks—units of sevens) (there were seven weeks [units of seven] listed before this sixty-two, for a total of sixty-nine) *shall Messiah* (the Anointed One) *be cut off/killed, but not for Himself ...And He* (Messiah) *shall confirm the covenant with many for one week* (during the final week) (unit of sevens)*; and in the midst/middle of the* (this final—70th) *week* (unit of sevens) *He* (Messiah) *shall cause the sacrifice and the oblation to cease."*

It is from these Scriptures we learn that Jesus (Messiah) would teach and minister for three and one-half years before He was crucified (cut off) in the midst/middle of the seventieth seven year period = 3 1/2 years. Jesus fulfilled this prophecy!

Jesus also fulfilled the portion which states, *"And He* (Messiah) *shall make, or confirm, or reaffirm the covenant,"* during the seventieth week (unit of seven) (490th year). This covenant is known and identified as the *New Testament* (covenant, compact, pact, treaty, convention or agreement).

"And in the midst of the (final seventieth) *week* (unit of seven) *He* (Messiah) *shall cause the sacrifice and the oblation/offerings to cease."*

We read in the *New Covenant* at Hebrews 10:8-18, *"Previously saying, 'Sacrifice and oblation, burnt offerings, and offerings for sin You* (God) *did not desire, nor had pleasure in them'* (which are offered according to the law), *then He* (Jesus) *said, 'Behold, I have come to do Your will, O God.' He* (God) *takes away the first* (sacrifices and oblations) *that He may establish the second. By that* (the second) *will we have been sanctified through the*

135

offering of the body of Jesus Christ once and for all. And (yet) *every priest stands ministering daily and offering repeatedly the same sacrifices, which can never take away sins. But this Man* (Jesus), *after He had offered one sacrifice for sins forever, sat down at the right hand of God, from that time waiting until His enemies are made His footstool. For by* **one** *offering* (oblation and sacrifice) *He* (Jesus) *has perfected forever those who are being sanctified. And the Holy Spirit also witnesses to us; for after He had said before: 'This is the* **covenant** *that I will make with them after those days, says the Lord: I will put My laws into their hearts, and in their minds I will write them,' then He adds: 'And their sins and their lawless deeds will I remember no more.' Now where there is remission of these sins, there is no longer an offering* (oblation or sacrifice) *for sin."*

The Scriptures make it very clear that the crucifixion and death of our Lord Jesus Christ made *all "sacrifices and oblations"* made by the law (contained in the Old Testament) no longer acceptable to God. They were rendered null and void, or canceled—that is, *"He caused the sacrifices and the oblations to cease."* Yet, the priest refused to accept the fact that their sacrifices and oblations were no longer acceptable to God (caused to cease) and continued to perform this empty ritual. Just like so many today, *"Having a form* (ritual) *of godliness, but denying the power thereof* (of God). *From such turn away!"* (2 Tim. 3:5).

Now you can see very clearly that the seventy weeks (units of sevens) *have been fulfilled*! No gap! We might have known there was no gap because in the *"seventy years of the desolation of Jerusalem,"* the example shown Daniel, there was *no proclaimed gap* between the sixty-ninth and seventieth years of the "desolation of Jerusalem." Certainly Gabriel would have told Daniel this also, since he hid none of the *horror* or *hope* that was to come.

If you accept the "gap" theory, you are "on the road to Emmaus." If Jesus came and walked with you, you may believe Him to be one of the "false Christs" of the end of this age. You would still be waiting for the seventy weeks of Daniel to be fulfilled!

Let us look at some other accepted false doctrines/theories that are based on Daniel 9:

Based on the "midst/middle" of the seventieth week, three and one-half (3 1/2) years of Daniel 9:26, some say is the same three and one-half (3 1/2) years (forty-two months = 3 1/2 years) of Revelation 13:5. By this distortion, they make our Lord Jesus Christ out to be the Anti-Christ! *"The beast was given a mouth to utter proud words and blasphemies and to exercize his authority for forty-two months* (3 1/2 years). *He opened his mouth to blaspheme God...All inhabitants of the earth shall worship the beast* (anti or false Christ) *all whose names have not been written in the book of life belonging to the Lamb..."* (Rev. 13:5-8, NIV).

Some then say the Anti-Christ makes a treaty (covenant) with Israel for seven years, but breaks the treaty in the midst/middle of that seventieth week of years. The Devil/Satan, the power of Mr. 666 (Rev. 13:2) does *not* make covenants. The word, *"covenant,"* in its Hebrew and Greek equivalents, appears three hundred-eighteen times in the Bible, and *not once* is it in association with the Devil/Satan or Anti-Christ. Our Lord Jesus Christ tells us that the Devil's ministry is *"...to steal, and to kill, and to destroy,"* (John 10:10), but not to make covenants. The "covenant" is made with *"many"* (who-so-ever) *not* Israel. In fact, Israel is not even mentioned in verses 24 through 27!

Some then say it is Anti-Christ that causes the sacrifices and oblations to cease as, *"he as God sitteth in the temple of God, shewing himself that he is God,"* (2 Thess. 2:4). More on this later in this chapter.

If you accept any one of the above three false doctrines, you have established events and situations that are to occur *before* the return of our Lord Jesus Christ, and you are "on the road to Emmaus."

On page 7 of the book, *"88 Reasons Why The Rapture Will Be In 1988"* we read "...that from the Day of Atonement 1988 through the Day of Atonement 1995 is the 70th week of Daniel. (This single fact is unchallengable proof that this book is correct and true.)" That is only one of many blinding doctrines of today contained in that false prophet's book.

The date he selected for the "rapture" was September 12, 1988. We can expect more "rapture" dates to be set between now and the year 2001...they also will be false alarms.

Another false doctrine which is widely taught and accepted is that the temple must be rebuilt in Jerusalem *before* Jesus returns. The cited Scriptures are Acts 15:16 and Amos 9:11, *"After this I will return and will build again the tabernacle of David."* We are told in 1 Chronicles 15:1 and 16:1, *"And David prepared a place for the ark of God* (of the covenant) *and pitched for it a tent."* The "tabernacle of David" was a tent, *not* a stone temple. But in this tent, all who came in to worship God had direct access to the ark of the covenant. It was not hidden in the Holy of Holies, into which only the high priest of the temple could enter, and that only once each year during the Day of Atonement/Yom Kippur. In Matthew 27:51, Mark 15:38 and Luke 23:45, we learn that when Jesus cried out from the cross and *"yielded up His spirit. Behold, the curtain/veil* (of the temple) *was torn in two from top to bottom,"* giving direct access to the "mercy seat of God," which was the ark of the covenant in the Holy of Holies. Remember, the Feast of Tabernacles finds its parallel or counterpart in the Holy of Holies containing the ark of the covenant.

In 1 Chronicles 15 and 16, this *"Tabernacle of David"*

was filled with music and praise. Praise is being restored into the worship of our Lord today where the Holy Spirit is free to lead the worshipers to worship Him in Spirit and in Truth. In John 4:23, 24 Jesus says, *"...the true worshippers shall worship the Father in spirit and in truth: for the Father seeketh such to worship Him. God is a spirit and they that worship Him must worship Him in spirit and in truth."*

But the most obvious thing about the "new temple," is contained in Revelation, chapter 21. However, let us first look at the scripture from Amos 9:11, *"In that day will I raise up the tabernacle of David that is fallen..."* and Acts 15:16, *"After this I will return, and will build again the tabernacle of David, which is fallen down."*

In the Old Testament, Amos prophesied, and in the New Testament, Jesus confirmed that *He, God*, would rebuild the temple—no earthly man *could* build the kind of new temple that Jesus is talking about, because in Rev. 21:2, 3 we read, *"And I, John, saw the holy city, **new Jerusalem**, coming down **from God** out of heaven, prepared as a bride adorned for her husband. And I heard a great voice saying, '**Behold the tabernacle of God is with men**, and He will dwell with them, and they shall be His people, and **God Himself shall be with them**, and be their God!'"*

Hallelujah! Isn't that exciting!

But what about the "temple" of 2 Thessalonians 2:3, 4? *"Let no one **deceive you** by **any means**; for that Day of Christ will not come unless the **falling away** come first, and the **man of sin is revealed**, the son of perdition, who opposes God and exults himself above all that is called God, or that is worshipped; so as God he sits in the **temple** of God showing himself that he is God,"* (NKJ).

First, let us look at the word, *temple* in the original Greek text from which this passage was translated. In the New Testament, there are two Greek words that translate into the one English word, temple: *Hieron*—a priestly edifice of wood, stone and mortar and *Naos*—a dwelling place, inner sanctuary.

Hieron is used seventy-one times and is consistent with the following Scriptures: Matthew 21:12, Mark 11:15, Luke 19:45 and John 2:15, *"When Jesus came to Jerusalem, He went into the temple (hieron) of God and drove out all those who bought and sold in the temple (hieron), and overturned the tables of the money changers and the seats of those who sold doves."*

Naos is used in the following Scriptures: John 2:19 and 21, *"Jesus...said unto them* (the Jews), *'Destroy this temple (naos), and in three days I will raise it up...'"* He was speaking of the temple *(naos)* of His body.

1 Corinthians 3:16, *"Do you not know that you are the temple (naos) of God and that the Spirit of God dwells in you? If anyone defiles the temple (naos) of God,* God will destroy him. For the *temple (naos) of God is holy, which temple (naos) you are."*

1 Corinthians 6:19, *"Do you not know that your body is the temple (naos) of the Holy Spirit who is in you, whom you have from God, and you are not your own?"*

2 Corinthians 6:16, *"What agreement has the temple (naos) of God with idols? For you are the temple (naos) of the living God. As God has said, 'I will dwell in them and walk among them. I will be their God, and they shall be My people.'"*

Acts 7:48, *"The most High God does not dwell in temples made with hands."* (Also referred to in 2 Chron. 2:6, *"But who is able to build Him a house, seeing the heaven and heavens cannot contain Him?"*)

Acts 17:24, *"God, who made the world and everything in it, seeing He is Lord of heaven and earth, does not dwell in temples made with hands.* ''

The word, temple, in 2 Thessalonians 2:4, comes from the Greek word, *naos*, and may have nothing to do with a temple built "with hands" of wood, stone and mortar—Greek word—*hieron*.

To further understanding of what God is saying in this passage of Scripture we must look at the phrase, *"man of sin, son of perdition,"* which, like Revelation 13:16, refers to the beast as, "he." The translators assumed the "he," but are *not* justified by the original *Greek text*, where this passage is written in the *neuter gender*. Therefore, in the neuter gender the reference could be neither male nor female, or it can include *both* male and female. The book, *Theomatics* by *Jerry Lucus and Del Washburn of Stein and Day, Briarcliff Manor, New York 10510*, makes this, and much more, so very clear and concluded that, "the beast is a one-world system, which is to prevail during the tribulation period." The term, *"man of sin, son of perdition"* may be like referring to "the beast" of Revelation 13 as "he," and both terms include both male and female.

Perdition (Greek: *apoleia*) means destruction, and in the King James Version is translated into seven different English words: perdition—8, destruction—5, waste—2, damnation—1, damnable - 1, pernicious-way, and perish—1.

Hebrews 10:39, in the Amplified Bible, can give us insight into the meaning of the word, "perdition," *"Our way is not that of those who draw back* (return) *to eternal misery* (perdition) *and are utterly destrpyed, but we are of those who believe—who cleave to and trust in and rely on God through Jesus Christ, the Messiah—who have faith for the preserving of the soul."*

Now we understand in 2 Thessalonians 2:3, 4, the day of Christ will not come until a *"falling away"* of believers (if they were not believers, they could not "fall away" or depart from the faith). Daniel speaks of this day in chapter 11, verse

35 prophesying (Amplified Bible), *"And some of those who are wise, prudent and understanding* (believers) *shall be weakened and fall* (away)*; thus then the insincere among the people will lose courage and become deserters. It will be a test to refine, to purify and make those among* (God's people) *pure, even unto the time of the end; because it is yet for a time* (God) *appointed."* Can you doubt that this prophecy is being fulfilled today?

In this *"falling away"* purging, cleansing, and purifying of the composite/corporate body of the Lord Jesus Christ, those (male and female) of sin will *"be revealed"* along with those (males and females) headed for destruction (perdition), that they may confess their sin *before* falling into eternal damnation (perdition).

They sit in their physical bodies (the temple of God), opposing God (not led by the Holy Spirit, but depending on their own reasonings) and exalting themselves in this temple (their body) to the satisfaction of the ego, even exalting themselves above God, who is to be worshiped. Sitting in their bodies (temples) proclaiming themselves to be God. They have *"fallen away"* into the world's trap of *"I* will do all things *my* way, to my pleasure and to *my* glory." Thus, they are saying, *"I* am God and ruler in this temple, *my* body, by the power of *my* mind, will and intellect (soul)," *not* allowing God to reign by the power of His Holy Spirit.

While many use these Scriptures of 2 Thessalonians 2:3, 4 in their search for the Anti-Christ, it is right between our ears: our soul, mind, will and intellect. Some have spent more time looking for an Anti-Christ than for the Lord Jesus Christ. Jesus said *"He that is not with Me is against me,"* (Anti-Christ), Matthew 12:30.

I hope you know there is not one single Scripture calling or naming a *man* Anti-Christ! The word, Anti-Christ, only appears five times in the whole Bible. Those Scriptures, 1 John 2:18 and 22, 4:3 and 2 John 7, make clear that

Anti-Christ is a *spirit*.

So, if you are looking for the temple to be rebuilt in Jerusalem for the Anti-Christ to sit in and proclaim himself to be God, you are "on the road to Emmaus."

The false doctrine with the most potentially damaging effect to Christians alive at the "end of the age," is the rapture (the physical removal of Biblical Christians from the earth to heaven).

In these "end of the age" times, Scriptural revelations are coming rapidly, and with increasing rapidity as "the pain/pangs of child birth" and in the fulfillment of His promise in Daniel 12:4 (Amplified Bible), *"But you, O Daniel, shut up the words and seal the book until the time of the end.* (Then) *men shall run to and fro and search anxiously* (through the Book)*, and knowledge* (of God's purposes as revealed by His prophets) *shall be increased and become great."* I believe we are in those days and these days are described in Amos 8:11, *"Behold, the days come, saith the Lord God, that I will send a famine in the land, not a famine of bread, nor a thirst for water, but* (a famine for) *of hearing the words of the Lord."* The blessing is that our understanding of God's Word will increase, but we must rid ourselves of these many blinding doctrines which *"...changed the truth of God into a lie..."* (Rom. 1:25). The rapture lie becomes obvious when we review "the truth of God's Word."

Jesus prayed, *"Father do not take the believers out of the world, but keep them from the evil one,"* (John 17:15 and 20). Can you find a Scripture where Jesus prays, "Father take the believers out of the world?" If not, then you can be very sure that His prayer will be answered and fulfilled!

Jesus teaches us that before or at *"the coming of the Son of Man, the wicked will be taken* (converted or destroyed) *from among the just,* (righteous)*"* in Matthew

13:41, 48 and 49, 24:37-41 and Luke 17:26-30.

Can you find five Scriptures where Jesus says the just, righteous or believers will be taken from among the wicked or evil? If not, you can be very sure that Jesus is *not* a false prophet!

God confirms the words of Jesus in Psalm 145:20 and Proverbs 2:21, 22 and 10:30, **"The upright** (righteous) **shall dwell in the land** (world)**, and the perfect shall remain in it. But, the wicked** (evil) **shall be cut-off from** (tares) (destroyed) **the earth, and the transgressors shall be rooted out of it."**

Can you find three Old Testament Scriptures where God says the righteous will be removed from the world/earth? If not, you can be very sure that God is *not* a liar! Nor does He make "mistakes." Nor does He "neglect to mention" a few things that men need to "fill in" for Him! He has told us *everything* we need to know, it is our *duty* to search the scriptures and *see* if "these things be true!"

A recent example of how the rapture doctrine keeps one from seeing an "end of the age" truth/revelation, is a man who said God revealed to him, "that only those who had received the Holy Spirit baptism would be in the next move of God." He has an extensive television and convention ministry where he teaches, "that only the Holy Spirit baptized Christians will be caught up in the rapture." This error has been accepted by other rapture pastors and teachers who have spread this lie to others. We have previously discussed the revelation that God is moving in the pattern of the Hebrew Feasts and God's next (or present) move is the fulfillment foretold by the Feast of Tabernacles (the last Hebrew Feast) where the Biblical Christians will be transformed, transfigured, changed or glorified.

If you still believe there will be a rapture, you are surely "on the road to Emmaus," and if Jesus came to walk with you, you would not recognize Him because you are blinded

144

by the doctrine that you are to be ''caught up'' to return to earth with Him.

Stay off ''the road to Emmaus,'' *''search the Scriptures daily to see if these things be true,''* (Acts 17:11). And *''receive with meekness the implanted/ingrafted word*** (of God)*, which is able to save your soul,''* (James 2:21).

11

Consequences Of The Rapture Doctrine

The sad consequences of the rapture doctrine are many, the following are a few of them:

1. The rapture doctrine, by implication, says, "Accept Jesus as the Savior of your spirit and go to heaven if you die, or fly away to heaven if still alive." It makes heaven your "blessed hope" and creates a *false* security that you will be removed from the earth before the "great tribulation." This places you in an excellent position and condition to be among those believers who will be victims of the *"great falling away."* They were not prepared to *go through* as *overcomers*. God might well see them as being "lukewarm" (Revelation 3:16).

2. The rapture robs you of attaining the full and complete salvation God has promised and prepared for you. Those having attained spirit salvation by accepting Jesus as their Savior have been taught "they have it all," and will receive their reward in heaven. Scriptures do *not* say that. Then those who

have accepted Jesus as their Holy Spirit baptizer for the salvation of their soul are taught "they have it all," and that they may be the only ones to receive "the blessed hope"—the rapture. But God tells us in many Scriptures and by the prophetic Hebrew Feasts and the life of our Lord Jesus Christ that there is also a body salvation available through accepting Jesus as Lord. How very sad it is to stop short of so great and complete a salvation—spirit, soul and body—by accepting the lie of rapture.

Knowing that *full* and complete salvation includes spirit, soul and body, when I am asked (often antagonistically), "Are you full-Gospel?" my answer is, "As near as I can tell, I am somewhat less than two-thirds of being full Gospel!" (I have the spirit and soul rebirth, I am waiting for a better body!)

Do not let the lie of rapture cause you to stop short of *All* that God has promised and reserved for you *through* and *in* Jesus Christ the Lord.

3. As important as it is for each of us to go on to receive the fullness of the promises of God through Jesus Christ the Lord, it is essential to the completion of the corporate body of Christ to *"bring forth the one perfect man,"* (Eph. 4:13). Will you go on to completeness and the fullness of Christ, or will you stop short of that true "blessed hope" (Christ in you, the hope of glory) and be in the great "falling away" with the rapture doctrine and other false doctrines being taught by various groups?

4. There is also another sad consequence of rapture. We are told in Hebrews 11 (God's Hall of Faith) that these great men and women cannot *"come in to perfection or completeness without us."* Hebrews 11:39 through 12:2, in the New International Version, *"These were all commended for their faith, yet none of them received what had been promised. God had planned something better for us so that **only together with us** would they be made*

147

perfect, (spirit, soul and body).

"Therefore, since we are surrounded by such a great cloud of witnesses, let us throw off everything that hinders and the sin that so easily entangles, and let us run with perseverance the race marked out for us. Let us fix our eyes on Jesus the Author (Originator) *and Perfecter of our faith, who for the joy set before Him endured the cross, scorning the shame, and sat down at the right hand of the throne of God."*

If the realization that the perfection and completion of these great people of faith depends on us attaining the fullness of *"what had been promised"* by God, does not humble us and consume us with the desire to *"run the race that is marked out for us,"* I do not know what it will take to fill us with that desire and purpose! In these verses we are commanded to *"throw off everything that hinders"* our running this race unto perfection and completeness in spirit, soul and body. If we truly love Jesus and all He has done for us, are we not then willing to suffer and die, if that is required of some of us, just as *He* and so many thousands of His followers already *have*? Can we admit to Jesus we *would* be willing? Can we truly not *trust* Him to see us *through* the "valley of the shadow of death" and "love not our lives unto the death..."?

5. The rapture may cause believers to fulfill the accusation that "you are so heavenly minded that you are no earthly good." Many believers are detached from national and world events. They won't even *unite* to protect their own rights as Christian citizens, allowing atheistic Humanism to replace Christianity in the public (government) schools. The Supreme Court has ruled that Humanism *is* a religion. It is now *the* religion taught and protected in the government (public) schools. Students have the right to have and read pornographic, obscene and filthy material on campus, but do not have the right to carry or read Bibles nor mention

148

the name of Jesus Christ our Lord in speeches. Some schools even offer courses in witchcraft.

If Christians are not going to get involved in politics at all levels of government, then those of the evil one (the Devil/Satan) control by default.

When a Christian does respond to the Lord's charge to *"occupy till I come (return)"* by seeking positions in government, many believers refuse to support and vote for them "because we don't believe the way he/she does," or even more perplexing, "men of God have no business running for office!"

I hope you will become informed, pray and take action. In the past, most actions of believers were based on ignorance of the true situation (knowing only what the controlled media told them) and prayer was seldom followed by action. There are many outstanding newsletters that will give you the truth about what is really going on, like: *Research Publications, P.O. Box 84902, Phoenix, AZ 85071,* or call *(602) 252-4477* and ask for a list of their newsletters. One of their best for world and national events, is *"Daily News Digest."*

6. To create, support, propagate and perpetuate the rapture, Holy Scriptures have to be ignored, distorted, taken out of context and corrupted. Thus, they are precluded from anything approaching the true revelations that God has for the end of this age. They reject *"the Spirit of Truth, and* (accept) *the spirit of error,"* (1 John 4:6). It can be said that the little leaven of a lie will leaven the whole loaf (Scriptural understanding). Saint Peter states it even more forcefully in 2 Peter 3:16 (Amplified Bible), *"...Even as our beloved brother Paul also wrote to you according to the spiritual insight given him, speaking of this as he does in all his letters. There are some things in those* (epistles of Paul) *that are difficult to understand, which the ignorant and unstable twist and misconstrue to their own utter destruction, just as* (they distort and

misinterpret) **the rest of the Scriptures."** We have shown what the escapists have done and do to Paul's first letter to the Thessalonians chapter 4 verse 17, to establish the rapture.

My challenge to anyone or any group who believes the "rapture," is to prove me wrong by Scripture, *not* by what Reverend, Pastor or Doctor so-and-so says, but *by Scripture*. If anyone can show me, Scripture by Scripture, to be wrong on the rapture doctrine, their reward is $10,000 (ten thousand dollars).

The next chapter is "The $10,000 Challenge."

If anyone ever says that I am wrong and in error on the subject of "rapture," ask them how they spent the $10,000!!

12

The $10,000 Challenge!

The following Scriptures state clearly (requiring no interpretation) there will be *no* rapture (the physical removal of Biblical Christians from the world/earth to heaven). I will pay **$10,000** to anyone or any group who will list and quote an **equal** number of Scriptures that state **as clearly** there will be a "rapture."

1) Jesus prayed in John 17:15 and 20, *"I pray **not** that you* (Father God) *should take them* (believers: verse 20) ***out** of the world, but keep them from evil."* Do you doubt that the prayers of Jesus Christ our Lord will be answered/fulfilled?

2) Jesus tells us in Matthew 13:29-40, *"I shall **first** gather the tares from among the wheat."* The field is the world, the wheat represents the children of the Kingdom, the tares are the children of the Devil and the harvest is the end of this age.

3) Jesus also explains in Matthew 13:41, *"The Son of man*

shall send forth his angels, and they shall gather **out**
of his Kingdom all things that offend (evil), and them
which do iniquity."

4) Jesus continues to emphasize His point in Matthew
13:47-48, *"Again... they cast the bad/evil/wicked away
at the end of the age."*

5) Jesus states this point so very clearly in Matthew 13:49,
*"...At the end of the age, the wicked shall be taken from
among the just* (righteous). *"* Even after all these examples,
Jesus asks us in verse 51, *"Have you understood all these*
(parables) *taken together?"* (Amp.) Do we now understand
who is taken/destroyed out of the world at the end of the age?

6) Jesus is not a false prophet! In Matthew 24:37-41, Jesus
prophesies, saying, *"As the days of Noah were, so also
will the coming of the Son of Man be. For as in the days
of Noah before the flood*

They (the wicked) *were eating and drinking and*

They (the wicked) *were marrying and giving in marriage, until the day Noah entered the ark, and*

They (the wicked) *did not know until the flood came
and took*

Them all (the wicked) *away, so also will the coming
of the Son of Man. Then, at the coming of the Son of
Man, two men will be in the field, the* (wicked) **one** *will
be taken and the* (righteous) *one left. Two women will
be grinding at the mill, the* (wicked) *one will be taken
and the* (righteous) *one left."*

7) In Luke 17:26-30 and 34-37 we read, *"As it was in
the days of Noah, so it will be also in the days of the
coming of the Son of Man:*

They (the wicked) *ate,*

They (the wicked) *drank,*

They (the wicked) *married,*

They (the wicked) *were given in marriage until the day
that Noah entered the ark, and then the flood came and*

destroyed

Them all (the wicked). *Likewise also as it was in the days of Lot:*

They (the wicked) *ate,*

They (the wicked) *drank,*

They (the wicked) *bought,*

They (the wicked) *sold,*

They (the wicked) *planted,*

They (the wicked) *built; but the same day that Lot went out of Sodom* (not out of the world) *it rained fire and brimstone from heaven and destroyed them all* (the wicked). *Even so will it be in the day the Son of Man is revealed...'I tell you, in that night there will be two men in one bed, the* (wicked) *one will be taken and the* (righteous) *one left. Two women will be grinding together, the* (wicked) *one will be taken and the* (righteous) *one left. Two men will be in the field, the* (wicked) *one will be taken and the* (righteous) *one left.' And His disciples asked Him, 'Where, Lord* (will the wicked be taken)*?' And He answered them saying, 'Wheresoever the* (dead) *body is, there the vultures and buzzards be gathered together.'''* (Remember Rev. 19:17-18, where an angel calls the *"fowls that fly"* to devour the dead who rebelled against God.)

8) Peter confirms this truth for us in 2 Peter 2:5, "God saved (kept safe) *Noah...bringing the flood upon the ungodly of the world."* Noah was *not* taken out of the world.

9) Jesus emphasizes His point that the righteous ones are *NOT* taken out of the world in Matthew 24:21-22 and Luke 13:19-20 saying, *"If the days* (duration) *of the great tribulation were not shortened* (decreased in number), *no man* (flesh) *would survive* (be saved)*: But for the sake of the elect* (Biblical Christians) *those days will be shortened* (decreased in number)*."* Jesus makes it so very clear that

153

Biblical Christians will *go through* the great tribulation, since the Bible makes it clear that *all* the wicked will be *destroyed*, God wouldn't need to *"shorten the days of tribulation"* if only the wicked are there!

10) The 23rd Psalm repeats this message clearly, *"Yea, though I walk **through** the **valley of the shadow of death**, I will fear no evil; for **Thou art with me...**"*

11) Psalm 37:9-11, 28 & 29, *"The evildoers* (the wicked) *shall be destroyed* (cut off): *But those who wait* (endure) *upon the Lord shall **inherit the world/earth**. For yet a little while, and the wicked shall not be; yea, thou shalt diligently consider his place, and it shall not be. But the **meek** shall **inherit the earth**; and shall delight themselves in the abundance of peace...For the Lord loveth judgement, and forsaketh not His saints; they are preserved forever: but the seed of the wicked shall be cut off. The **righteous shall inherit the land, and dwell therein forever.**"*

12) Psalm 145:20, *"The Lord preserveth **all** them that love Him: But **all** the wicked He will destroy."*

13) Psalm 125:1, *"They that trust in the Lord shall be as* (like) *Mount Zion which **cannot be removed**, but shall **stay forever.**"*

14) Proverbs 10:30, *"The righteous shall **never** be removed: but the wicked shall **not** inhabit the earth."*

15) Proverbs 2:21-22, *"For the upright shall dwell in the land* (earth) *and the perfect shall **remain** in it, but the wicked shall be **cut off** (destroyed) **from the earth**, and the **transgressors** shall be rooted out of it."*

16) All the above Scriptures are combined and amplified in Psalm 37:34-40, *"Wait on the Lord, and keep His way, and He shall exault thee to **inherit the land**: when the wicked are **cut off** (tares) (destroyed), **thou shalt see it**. I have seen the wicked in great power, and spreading himself like a green bay tree* (that groweth in its own soil).

Yet he passed away, and, lo, he was not; yea, I sought him, but he (the wicked) **could not be found. Mark** *the perfect man, and behold the upright: for the end of that man is peace. But the transgressors shall be destroyed together: the end of the wicked shall* **be cut off***. But the salvation of the righteous is of the Lord: He is their strength in the* **time of trouble** (tribulation). *And the Lord shall* **help them***, and deliver them from the wicked (evil one) and* **save them***, because they* **trust in Him***."*

To understand what 1 Thessalonians 4:13-18 really tells us, read Chapter 5:

17) 1 Thessalonians 5:23-24, *"May the God of peace make you holy through and through. May you be kept sound in* **spirit, mind** *and* **body***, blameless* **until** *the coming of the Lord Jesus Christ. He who called you is utterly faithful and He will* **finish** *what He has set out to do,"* (PME).

Amen and Amen!

H. Speed Wilson
C/O Daring Books
913 Tuscarawas St. N.W.
Canton, OH 44702

P.S. Reproduction and distribution of this $10,000 challenge is approved and encouraged.

In the interest of promoting *gospel truth*; Daring Books will consider *publishing* any book which answers, point by point, chapter by chapter, *irrefutable scripture* proving and supporting a "rapture doctrine," without changing or distorting or ignoring *each* of the scriptures clearly stated in Colonel Wilson's book.

Index

158

159